Dialogue in a Major Key

Dialogue in a Major Key

Women Scholars Speak

Edited by

Mary H. Maguire
McGill University

National Council of Teachers of English
1111 W. Kenyon Road, Urbana, Illinois 61801-1096

Staff Editors: Michelle Sanden Johlas and Sheila A. Ryan

Cover Design: Barbara Yale-Read

Interior Design: Doug Burnett

NCTE Stock Number: 08814-3050

It is the policy of NCTE in its journals and other publications to provide a forum for the open discussion of ideas concerning the content and the teaching of English and the language arts. Publicity accorded to any particular point of view does not imply endorsement by the Executive Committee, the Board of Directors, or the membership at large, except in announcements of policy, where such endorsement is clearly specified.

Library of Congress Cataloging-in-Publication Data

Dialogue in a major key : women scholars speak / edited by Mary H.
  Maguire.
       p.   cm.
    Includes bibliographical references and index.
    ISBN 0-8141-0881-4 (pbk.)
    1. English philology—Study and teaching.   2. English teachers—
Interviews.   3. Women teachers—Interviews.   4. Women scholars—
Interviews.   I. Maguire, Mary H., 1943-   .   II. National Council
of Teachers of English.
PE65.D53   1995
428'.007—dc20   95-3985
                                                                  CIP

Contents

Acknowledgments

This book was created out of conversations. I am grateful to a number of individuals who collaborated with me in the construction of this intertextual endeavor. I want to thank Jane Christensen, who promptly replied to my initial letter of inquiry about the possibility of such a text with a personal note of encouragement and enthusiasm for such an endeavor. I appreciate Michael Spooner's consistent and positive support, his valuable advice, and enthusiastic response to the draft prospectus. I also appreciate his patience and accessibility; the project has taken longer than we planned. I also want to thank the anonymous reviewers who read the initial prospectus and provided many thoughtful ideas and useful recommendations. In addition, I appreciate the care, attention, and support of two interim senior editors, Michelle Sanden Johlas and Marlo Welshons, as well as Sheila Ryan, project editor, in bringing this manuscript into production.

I also appreciate the commitment, time, and insight of Barbara Graves, a Ph.D candidate at McGill University, who assumed the task of editing and proofreading this text seriously and with friendship and understanding.

I have enjoyed collaborating with you, my conversational partners, and appreciate your willingness to participate in the initial interviews, providing me and the readers with a dialogue of substance and style. I am grateful for the good humor with which you revisited your texts and became excited about extending the conversation. Thank you for enriching my life and expanding my thinking about issues that concern all English teachers. You opened up worlds to me through our conversations and have become—in the Maori sense of the word *whanau*—my extended professional family.

Prologue: Opening Conversations

This book is about conversations with nine, well-known international women scholars whom I interviewed at different times and in different contexts. As Gadamer observes, conversations have a sort of spirit of their own. One cannot determine, in advance, whither they will lead:

> A conversation is a process of two people understanding each other. Thus, it is characteristic of every true conversation that each opens him/herself to the other person, truly accepts his/her point of view as worthy of consideration and gets inside the other to such an extent that he/she understands not a particular individual, but what he/she says. (Gadamer 1984, 347)

Certainly, the conversations in this book have a spirit of their own, as do the voices you will hear.

Nine contributors—Yetta Goodman, Margaret Gill, Margaret Meek Spencer, Janet Emig, Aviva Freedman, Henrietta Dombey, Elody Rathgen, Patricia Symmonds, and Louise Rosenblatt—present their views of reality as they talk with me about issues in language and learning, teacher education, schooling, and society within and across social, political, national, and linguistic boundaries. Each conversation has its own situated context, beginning, and "opening move," to borrow a metaphor from Margaret Meek Spencer. As she remarks: "We have all lived through in our different cultures nearly a half a century of social and educational change."

Since the first International Dartmouth Seminar on the Teaching of English, there has been an increasing recognition, in the field of English education in many countries, of the need for ongoing international dialogue. This international movement in English education has largely been accomplished through journal publications and at national and international conferences such as NCTE, CCTE, AATE, NZATE, NATE, IFTE. However, little has been published in the way of indepth remarks and reflections of key women scholars about issues and concerns that either, in the words of former IFTE president Margaret Gill, "unite or divide us as a Profession." This book proposes to do just that. It presents conversations and reflections of these international scholars from Australia, Canada, England, the United States, New Zealand, and Barbados at a particular moment in our and their professional histories. The contributors to this volume serve the profession by their international legacies—icons of speaking personalities, reflecting, looking back, and looking ahead to matters that concern all English teachers.

These conversations began in 1986 when I was an associate editor and columnist of the "Reflections" section of the journal *Reading Canada Lecture.* In this section, I asked scholars and educators to reflect upon the Canadian and international educational scene with particular reference to reading and language education, but also more broadly on the issues that they see as interesting or critical in education generally. In all the interviews I conducted between 1986 and 1990 in this editorial role, individual scholars, both male and female, moved beyond the immediacy of the Canadian or American educational scene to diverse international contexts and concerns, thus suggesting a less parochial and more expansive view of the international borders of discourse.

My initial interviews with Gill, Dombey, Spencer, Emig, and Freedman were not preplanned or structured, or even conceptualized as a book during the times I talked with them. When I assumed responsibility as co-editor for the column in *Reading Canada Lecture,* I engaged a new genre for this section of the journal—the conversational interview. I envisioned this genre then, and now appreciate it more clearly, as being dialogic in character and capable of capturing human voices and speaking personalities. The interviews in this book are deliberately open-ended and informal, minimally edited and not just simply tape-recorded, transcribed, spliced, and cut. Each was a surprise—always a new conversation leading to a new beginning in my own thinking and opening up further conversations with these women and other colleagues and above all consolidating a sense of trust and respect.

All nine women responded positively and enthusiastically to my invitations to "interview them" and tell me and the readers about their personal reactions to current issues in language and literacy, recent developments in theory and research, and the politics of education. Each initially asked me *what I wanted her to talk about.* I deliberately begged the question, and readers will note that in the opening moves of our conversations I usually start with a general focus and let the conversation naturally unfold. These women speak to teachers and teacher educators and take strong critical perspectives on issues; they are neither quiet nor silent voices (Belenky, Blythe, Goldberger, and Tarule 1986). They speak from a position of strength and commitment to teachers and learners and reveal themselves as learners and teachers. Their dialogues represent the kind of thoughtful exchanges which our conferences and national associations need to foster, encourage, and support.

Readers will notice topical shifts in the conversations, which is natural in open-ended conversations, and even shifts in perspectives with some of them as they revisit their transcribed, written texts a few years later. However, through these conversations, we can see the merits of a view of the linguistic process as being personal and heuristic and necessarily social, exploratory, and political. Each speaker tells her own educational story and expresses her own voice. However, a common thread runs throughout their conversations, both in the concerns they voice and their ways of talking about research, teaching, and learning. Read together, they can tell an interesting international story of English teaching. The conversations with Margaret Gill, Janet Emig, and Henrietta Dombey were conducted when these participants were closely linked with the IFTE and were serving as national presidents of their associations (AATE, NCTE, and NATE). Elody Rathgen was serving as president of the IFTE when we talked. I hope that these conversations serve more than the archival value that is obvious. The phrase "Opening Conversations" covers for me the diversity of our exchanges and their forms in our dialogues with ourselves and others.

There are many ways to read this book. It draws on the personal experiences and critical perspectives of these women scholars as they talk about issues that concern them at a time in our history when curricula and tests designed by states and provinces are being mandated in several states, provinces, and countries and when school populations around the world are becoming increasingly multicultural. While the various contributors talk from within the perspectives of their international settings, their discussions are truly international in interest and application and may be viewed as historically, politically situated discourse and dialogues. Some readers might want to explore the concept of conversational circle and the conversations themselves as interpersonal talk and ways of coming to know and understand. Others may be interested in the variety of issues and positions that emerge in our discussions. Still others may see potential in opening up contestable issues and debating them further. Some may value and engage in reflecting upon the conversations as a collaborative philosophical inquiry and examining them in relation to teaching and learning as modes of inquiry and approaches to it.

Margaret Meek Spencer calls my endeavor an intertextual initiative. Structurally, I have divided each contributor's text into three parts. In the first part, I set the scene for each interview. Here I include a personal text and context before each interview, situating the time and circumstance of each interview. The second part includes the actual edited interview. Each contributor was asked to reread her interview and make any editorial changes, knowing that I wanted to preserve the conversational flavor of our opening conversations. The third part presents each individual's retrospective commentary on her own interview. All of the participants had access to all of the other interviews and were invited to reflect and comment on their own interview as well as those of the others.

In my initial prospectus for this book, I had intended to write a separate chapter on intertwined conversations within a Bakhtinian theoretical framework. Thanks to an anonymous reviewer who argued for less editorial apparatus, I have not done that. The reviewer wrote the following: "If theoreticians like Bakhtin, Bruner and Maguire are right then the interviewees are quite capable of speaking for themselves." This decision I hope will allow all readers to discover and create their own intertextual ties with the texts and the voices. I invite readers to play with and to capture what James Britton has called the multiple layers of dual and triple talk that can occur in collective monologues and dialogues, for example when children speak to themselves and others while playing with ideas, formulating and reformulating their thoughts.

Last but not least, I had asked Louise Rosenblatt to write an epilogue. In my initial conversation with her about negotiating her part in the book, she stated that she preferred to hold another conversation rather than, in her words, "put final closure on these individuals' thoughts." In our conversation, "Looking Back and Looking Forward," she reopens the conversation, and *evocation* becomes once again a key word in continuing the international dialogue. She provides us with a new metaphor for listening to different voices and harmonizing within and across diverse communities.

Yetta M. Goodman

Defining Ourselves and Our Students as Literate

In a commentary for the *Whole Language Umbrella Newsletter* (1991–1992, 1), Susan Elliot demonstrates how she defines herself as a teacher and a literate language user and how she helps her students define themselves in a similar vein:

> Whenever possible, I write alongside my students and we share our results, frustrations, successes and failures together. . . . I also talk to them about the books I am reading myself, orally and in response to their reading journals, my purposes for reading . . . and they in turn bring in titles they have enjoyed and share them with me.

Susan demonstrates the importance of teachers sharing what they do and who they are with their students. She not only helps students come to know and define her as a teacher, but she comes to know her students through their own words and transactions with the world. Individuals are encouraged to let others know how they define themselves, to wonder about how others see them, and in this way to continue their own growth in language and language use.

As I read the provocative conversations between the outstanding teacher educators represented in this book, I was again drawn to a notion of what it means to define oneself as a literate language user, as a teacher, and as a learner. Each interview allows readers to see how these women define themselves: within the profession, as teachers and teacher educators, as women, and as knowledgeable about learning, teaching, and language. But each conversation also shows how these women express in the most respectful terms ways of defining others with whom they work, be they teachers or students.

This concept of defining ourselves, our students, and literacy is one I have been considering a good deal of late as it has become obvious to me that what we count as literacy, who we count as literate, the language we use as we talk about the literacy and learning of others, and how we help to define literacy are crucial to its teaching and learning. Such definitions have profound effects on how students and teachers see themselves and define themselves as literate human beings in a literate society. Do they consider themselves readers or writers in control of their learning or inadequate as readers or writers? Do they perceive themselves as teachers who are professional decision makers in control of their classrooms or as technicians?

I am fascinated when I listen to or read Denny Taylor's (1988) descriptions of what happens when the homeless and poor are asked to fill out forms that include questions such as "What is your address?" Without an address it is impossible to get a P.O. box, let alone social security benefits or job listings. Such experiences with institutionalized forms and rules define people as literate or not. Often they begin to define themselves reflecting the institutions' definitions.

Mike Rose in his book *Lives on the Boundary* (1989) has also helped me consider the concept of the literacy and learning definition of self. In his powerful study of the struggles and achievements of students on the boundaries of the literate world, Mike does not dwell on test score information or on the sensationalism of the illiteracy of certain groups in society. Rather, he tells their stories through their personal voices and at the same time tells his own story. Through Mike's research narrative, we discover how school and society can help the individual believe the label—I'm not a writer; I'm not a reader; I'm illiterate. But Mike also provides evidence that when institutions are organized to help people view their own purposes and functions for literacy and show them ways to discover their own literacy power, new worlds and opportunities open up and those involved begin to see themselves as literate human beings in new ways.

Vivian Paley (1989), a marvelous kindergarten teacher and author, adds to this concept when she discusses her reasons for writing down the conversations of the children in her kindergartens:

> To nourish this ongoing documentary, I have put away the scorecards and relearned what I once, as a child, could do quite well: make sense of the classroom by watching the children and listening to what they say. We are not, any of us, to be found in sets of tasks or lists of attributes; we cannot be defined or classified. We can be known only in the singular unfolding of our unique stories within the context of everyday events.

I don't want to argue that believing that one is a reader or writer will automatically make it so, although such an attitude goes a long way toward establishing a base of confidence for literacy learning. But I am convinced that when students believe they are not readers and writers, they act out those characterizations; in other words, they fulfill society's expectations.

Whenever I read studies of poor and good readers, I am aware of how these studies define readers. Test scores are used without any evaluation of the nature of the test. In most of these studies, if you examine the data carefully, you discover that both groups of readers are more similar than different. Yet the similarities are seldom addressed because it is not the quality of the learner and the learning being addressed but the definition of the specifics of a good or poor reader.

Marilyn Adams concludes, in *Beginning to Read* (1990), that students who learn to read must be phonologically aware through direct instruction. I happened to be reading both Marilyn's and Mike's books at the same time and realized that they were each describing similar populations. Yet because Marilyn and Mike chose different frames through which to view and describe these populations, they look like totally different social groups. Marilyn establishes what poor readers look like on the basis of standardized test scores and clinical research practices. Mike, on the other hand, allows the people in his research narrative to present themselves through personal histories—the stories of their lives. Literacy is seen as a part of their cultural and social experiences, and they define themselves through their own voices.

Dialogue in a Major Key provides many opportunities to explore how students and teachers define themselves and each other as literate users of language. Within each dialogue, Mary Maguire and her co-conversationalists offer their definitions—about themselves, about other teacher educators and teachers, about students, and about literacy—by exploring the socio-cultural contexts in which the teachers and students they work with live. Through their conversations, they reflect confidence in the knowledge that they have, but at the same time they present themselves as learners always tentative in their present knowledge, always wondering and asking new questions, ready to reevaluate their knowledge and beliefs. They also allow the voices of others to define themselves. All members of the dialogues show respect and belief in the potential and possibilities for the development of a critically literate society among their students and teachers with whom they work. However, concerns about the realities of schooling are not set aside in a simplistic way, but are addressed in terms of the realities of the political scene that faces teacher education and the teaching of English throughout the English language world. These women have the expertise and experience to be concerned with tough realities at the same time that they explore possibilities. Although the interviews have many themes in common, I will stay within this frame of the power of definition of literacy and what it means to be literate as I explore issues that highlight optimism, potential, and possibility as we move toward the twenty-first century.

Schools as Places for Change, for Optimism

Are schools places for change? What is the role that democracy plays in our concern for literacy learning? How does the way in which students and teachers define their roles in a literate world affect democracy and change in schools?

Henrietta Dombey raises a significant issue relating to the context in which students define themselves when she and Mary Maguire discuss the notion of "the democracy versus the autocracy." Henrietta argues that the enabling family is essentially a democratic family and suggests that we need to adapt this notion to the classroom. As students, at any level of education including university classes and programs, have control over their learning and become consciously aware of such control, their inquiries and opportunities to critique and to solve their problems are enhanced.

As a neophyte teacher years ago, I came to the education profession filled with enthusiasm and commitment to make changes in schools so that students would have opportunities different from mine in order to pursue a better life: opportunities to inquire into interesting problems, opportunities to become anything that they might want to be. My parents had made great sacrifices coming to the United States, seeking a democratic society in order to provide a better life for their children. Such optimism about democracy and education was built into my growing-up experiences. But in my teacher education program and often among some professional colleagues after that, I encountered a curious notion that seemed to be supported by some sociological and anthropological theories. Simply stated, such beliefs suggested that schools are established and organized to pass on the traditions of the society. According to this view, curriculum in schools should reflect the status quo; its purpose is not to produce change. Such notions are based on the belief that those in power have a vested interest in establishing and maintaining a society like the one in power. That's just the way things are supposed to be, and it is not the role of professional educators to rock the boat. Schools are not supposed to be progressive places where students and teachers consider questions about power issues related to race, ethnicity, gender, or socioeconomic status, nor are they places where controversial issues are raised by thoughtful teachers and students.

To this day, I have difficulty dealing with such conservatism among academic colleagues. Because of such status quo views, the voices of teachers, students, parents, and the community are not heard. I am tired of hearing children and adolescents being told they have poor vocabularies because their parents are immigrants and don't care about their educational experiences. I am tired of the simplistic reporting of testing programs that indicate that students cannot go to particular institutions or get into certain programs because of low test scores. I am tired of hearing that we should teach certain principles because they have always been taught that way.

I now understand that this dichotomy between schools as status quo institutions and schools as institutions for change and advancement for all members of society is a basis for volatile and significant disagreements in educational circles. There are those who want to pass on curriculum in the way it has been done for centuries. There are those who want schools to reflect what certain powerful individuals see as the successful products of an educational system.

It is uplifting to read the conversations by women who know that schools and educational institutions are places for hopes and dreams to be acted on and brought to fulfillment. In a variety of ways, these powerful voices demonstrate that institutions can become democratic places that make it possible for a range of people of color, belief systems, languages and cultures, finances and gender to discover hope, to fulfill dreams, and to change the nature of society for themselves, their children, and their children's children through the medium of language learning. In such institutions, students and teachers come to define themselves as learners. Louise Rosenblatt makes it clear that multiculturalism or cultural pluralism are possible only in a democratic society. Teachers are responsible to make learners proud of their heritage and to "also develop democratic values to honor and respect one another."

Mary discusses possible ways of achieving these opportunities when she raises the issue of harmonies in her interview with Henrietta and Louise. If we hope to allow students to discover the strengths in their personal learning histories, then educational institutions must work collaboratively with others to find much more dynamic ways of building harmonies between teacher education institutions and schools, homes and schools, communities and schools, especially in light of our multicultural world. Our tendency is to talk about cooperation with others. But in our school register, cooperation generally means that the others will do as we tell them to do. If they have their own ideas or are critical of what we ask of them, we usually declare that those persons or groups are not cooperative.

It is in the spirit of "harmonies," however, that we must be careful not to ignore the differences we have. Aviva Freedman cautions us not to sweep our differences under the rug. By allowing for healthy critique and debate, we can empower all the stakeholders in the educational experience to examine their particular views and find ways of presenting them and accommodating them to others. In this way, teachers, parents, and students come to believe that what they know and believe have value. They can begin to define who they are and what they believe as important within a democratic educational establishment. They each have unique contributions to make to others, but most especially to their own development. In this way, teachers move away from the transmission model of telling others, and teachers and students together discover ways of listening to each other and helping each other understand the various places each is coming from. Each discovers that personal ways of knowing have worth. They are therefore capable of defining themselves as successful users of language and literacy.

Elody Rathgen explores the importance of listening to the voices of students, parents, and teachers, while Patricia Symmonds explores issues of teachers and students building a sense of community. In a variety of ways, each of the women in this volume speaks to the importance of the development of democratic classrooms and schools in her own way. Democracy is not simply something to teach about, but it is a way to live daily in interactions with each other in the educational establishment. It is in democratic institutions that students and teachers define themselves as persons with control over their own learning histories.

Faith in Teachers and Students

How do we help teachers who are at the heart of what happens to language and literacy learning in the classroom develop democratic communities in their classrooms? How do we help them know that the more their students are involved in problem-solving opportunities, the more power both they and their students have to share? Margaret Meek Spencer addresses this when she states: "The minute we stop learning from teachers and children . . . we should just give up, because . . . we won't be of any use to either of them."

We have a long way to go to show widespread acceptance of the notion that, as students and teachers participate in a democratic learning environment, they will define themselves as literate users of language who take responsibility for their own language learning. Our colleagues in teacher education institutions are even more bound by transmission models of learning and teaching than elementary and secondary school teachers are. We need to look toward elementary and secondary school teachers who are already inviting their students and their parents to participate in curriculum development and collaborative inquiry for demonstrations of developing democratic classrooms at the tertiary level. As preservice and inservice teachers experience democracy in their own professional education, they are likely to be willing and able to establish similar experiences for the students in their classrooms.

All the interviews reflect the notion that children and teachers are always learners and learning. As teacher educators continue to learn from teachers and students, we can help them know the ways in which they contribute to the development of teacher education. Helping both teachers and students to define themselves as learners and as inquirers into the learning and teaching processes becomes a major objective of all school programs and teacher education institutions.

As a young teacher, although I was told by my administrators that I was a fine teacher, I did not view myself as the decision maker in my classroom. I looked to outsiders, to teacher educators as I received my master's degree, to books and articles authored by "researchers and scholars," to curriculum guides and district-level specialists. I was more than thirty years old when I finally began to define myself as a learner, to take responsibility for my own learning, to believe that I had something to offer to others, including my professors, about the learning that I was doing by interacting with the children and adolescents in my classroom.

Teachers need to be confident in the development of their professional sense. Through kid watching and sharing stories with their students as demonstrated by Susan Elliot and Vivian Paley, teachers come to know themselves and their students and become more relevant to their own and their students' learning. Teachers know more about the language and learning of students than anyone outside the classroom, except perhaps for parents. Teachers who become aware of their own *professional* sense, of how they are inquiring into their own classroom practices come to define themselves not as "just a teacher" but as a professional teacher, someone who knows what she is doing because of years of thinking, reading, self-reflecting, sharing ideas with others, and practicing. Teachers become aware that what they have been doing in their classrooms is inquiry into their own practices, a legitimate form of research, because they have used the questions they have about teaching and learning, read what others have had to say about these, and then applied their conclusions to their classroom settings to see if they work well or not. Such teachers are confident in their own decision making and are therefore willing to assume responsibility for such in the classroom.

All the interviewees focus on respect for the professionalization of teachers. In so doing, they legitimatize another important theme that allows for the development of a definition for becoming literate. Not only are there multiple paths to the literacy learning of students, but at the same time there are unique ways in which teachers come to know and work with their students. We have for too long tried to establish single pathways to literacy learning and teaching. Yet our established literature is full of stories about the many roads people have taken to becoming literate. Research provides evidence that people become literate in prisons and in schools; through reading books or reading the acknowledgments at the end of movies; through being read to a great deal at home; or through reading signs on stores, restaurants, and street corners.

We have for too long tried to establish a single effective teacher, hoping to clone this one type. We know too much about teachers and learners to continue such foolishness. We must allow for the many paths to learning and the many ways of knowing of teachers. This opens up the opportunity not only for the development of the democratic classroom, but for teachers to be at the forefront of innovation in their classrooms.

Elody focuses her interview on the concept of different voices. This was the theme for the IFTE conference in Auckland, New Zealand, but it is also reflected in recent books and magazines edited and written by teachers concerned with their own professionalism and opportunities for their students to come to know who they are and to believe in the power of their own literacy. Elody explores a powerful question: "Am I going to accept different students' voices, or am I going to take a bit of their voice away from them and give them some of the voice I would prefer to present?" She wonders if we really listen to the silent voices in our classrooms.

Aspects of the multiple ways of knowing are not only influenced by the different individual voices of students, but are also related to feminine issues in teaching and learning. The teaching force is becoming more female, especially at elementary and secondary levels, in recent years. We need to know more about how female ways of knowing influence language teaching and learning. Janet Emig addresses the feminine nature of teaching and teachers when she discusses the role of narrative. She believes that as female teachers, "We're initially more willing to trust the expressive mode. Consequently, emanating from that is a willingness to trust the role of narrative in thinking. We trust story and storying as a way of knowing more readily."

Both Janet and Margaret Spencer highlight the importance of respecting the multiple ways of knowing that are embodied by different teachers and students. Janet calls up Dewey when she urges us to trust what is emerging about what we are learning and about the legitimacy of many ways of knowing and to risk venturing forth into alternate ways of setting forth what we are learning. Henrietta cautions, however, that it is possible in the present climate of evaluation to establish "a tremendous spirit and determination amongst the teachers that their work should not be distorted or misrepresented by inappropriate assessments."

With the use of narrative, teachers can represent their own teaching practices and their professional ways of knowing. Narrative also provides many opportunities to hear about the ways in which people define themselves as literate. If we listen carefully to these stories, we will discover a good deal more about the many roads to literacy and the many ways of knowing.

Literacy and the Celebration of Diversity

What counts as literacy? Who is literate? How do we come to define our own literacy? It is important in elementary and secondary school teaching and in teacher education programs to understand that how communities and schools view teachers and students provides a framework through which they view themselves as literate beings. Such views profoundly affect literacy teaching and learning.

I have worked with teachers who did not know that they had the right to question the curriculum they believed they were being forced to teach. Such teachers often tell me that no one in all their college or university programs had ever encouraged them to ask questions or helped them realize that they had legitimate questions and the responsibility (not only the right) to ask such questions. Such teachers often respond initially with anger, but as they begin to believe that they have the right to question, they begin to reflect on their teaching practices, become readers of professional research and literature, begin to question instructional manuals and educational research, share their new knowledge and insights into their teaching with others through oral and written presentations. At the same time, they start changing their teaching practices, providing opportunities for their students to participate in curriculum development and share in the power that such decision making demands.

All the interviewees reflect their concerns for the rights, privileges, and responsibilities of others in order to enhance such developments in school settings as they show their concern for the cultural diversity that is prevalent in our schools, but Aviva reminds us that "we have very different stances that are related to something other than diversity."

There is a tendency in this highly literate society of ours to view literacy in and of itself as a pinnacle of achievement. We transfer this notion to language itself, especially when academics come together to talk about the impact that language has on thinking and communication. But we all know, as the interviews and commentaries in this book demonstrate, that the power of language is in how it is used and the purposes to which it is put.

How we define ourselves as literate has to do with what influences any literacy event. Those influences include the ways in which different cultural groups view the importance of literacy and school, as well as what cultural groups count as literacy and learning.

My mother was a strong force in my life to highlight my interest in school and in literacy learning, even though she had had very little schooling in both the Russian *stetl* (village) where she lived and in the United States as a Yiddish-speaking immigrant. She knew literacy was important and encouraged me to go to the library regularly and tried to support me to adapt to the requirements of the school, although the latter did not always work well. I knew that it would be nice to go to college or to the university, and my mother also thought this would be a nice goal. But most important for her was for me to be employable. So she urged me to take typing and secretarial courses in high school so that I would have something to fall back on.

In my own household with my three daughters, we took it for granted that they would all go to university. This was never questioned by their father, by themselves, or by me. Different expectations and beliefs about the world of literacy and learning profoundly affected my daughters and me. I willingly worked my way through a neighborhood junior college, while each of my three daughters went off to a university that all members of the family selected with great care.

We need to understand a good deal more about cultural and institutional influences on the teaching and learning of literacy. Mike Rose, Nancie Atwell, Denny Taylor are providing us with research narratives and insights into these influences. The interviews in the book explore many more of the issues that need to be addressed. We need to understand the personal histories of readers and writers and what aspects of home and school influence their responses to literacy. We need to look at the variations of students within one cultural group to understand why such differences occur, and we need to look at those students who achieve in similar ways even when they are influenced by different cultural patterns. The scenery is a complex one, and we must avoid simplifying it in order to inquire into our questions. Not only by examining cultural differences will we begin to understand more, but also by respecting and understanding the language variations of the people with whom we work.

Elody challenges us with her statement: "There is a link between the death of a language and the death of a culture." And then she asks an important question related to my theme of defining oneself: "Where do I stand?" She describes her loving British grandmother who would say, "Oh Elody, don't speak like that, dear, you sound like a New Zealander," and the Maori people were saying, "We are the people who belong here. This is our place where we stand." So I ask myself, "Where do I stand?"

At the same time, Patricia, as she discusses the linguistic issues in Caribbean education, asks the reader to think globally about language: "Language has always been a part of identity, but what many people do not appear to understand is that language also has global implications." Although she strongly advocates that "there would be linguistic chaos if each island employed its own dialect" and that "we owe it to our children to encourage the highest standards of correct Standard English," she states that in oral presentations and in written dialogue children are allowed to use Creole in situations where nonstandard expression would be expected.

Margaret Gill also explores this issue as she describes listening to two teachers who gave their kids a chance to learn and celebrate their own dialect often considered deficient and that usually defined the students as deprived. Opportunity to see their own language as a vehicle for learning provides not only power but opportunity to define oneself as a language user. Margaret discusses the many voices she has listened to who suggest "the multitude of ways in which power can be more readily shifted to kids in our classrooms to make them autonomous learners."

How we respond to students whose language, whether a dialect or a second language, varies from some established standard is crucial to the learners' views of themselves. Because of my study of language, I eventually developed a confidence about my own language use, but my sister, a retired secondary school teacher and counselor, who came from the same Yiddish-speaking background as I did, to this day says she has a weak vocabulary and cannot express herself well in writing because of her bilingual background.

Conclusions

For those who have the power to place others in specified classrooms, in degree programs, in designated social programs to receive services of various kinds, the way we define the people we serve becomes crucial to the way they are viewed by society and often by themselves. The myths that become established within society about people and who they are have incredible social and financial impact on their lives.

I am especially concerned by what this means for children and adolescents who have to contend with two languages in the school settings in a country where monolingualism is considered the norm and therefore superior to bilingualism. Ironically it seems that only if one learns a foreign language in a school setting is there a value placed on second language learning. These populations are not defined as bilingual or second language learners, but as students who are learning a foreign language. The strengths of bilingual students are often masked as deficits and problems because we have not learned well enough to allow learners to show us who they are and to define themselves for us. We must learn to listen better to what our students are saying. We must learn to read between and beyond the lines of what they write to find their expressions of meaning and inquiry.

At the same time, I am concerned about the many teachers who have been convinced that they are unknowing, that the knowledge they need is in professional textbooks, journals, or the heads of those they consider "experts." There is much we can learn together.

Margaret Gill informs us that, in her discussions with teachers at important international conferences, it is not "the big names at the top of the pages; it's . . . the fact that they've sat with other teachers from other countries . . . talked together about what made teaching hard, and what made it good and what they could learn from each other." The conversations with the teacher educators in this book indeed reveal how we learn from each other, but each of the voices also shows what members of the English education community can *do* and the contributions that they make in response to what we learn.

I was reminded as I wrote the quotation from Margaret Gill that learning and my sense of being active in advancements in educational settings came from sitting with others and talking about what makes teaching hard and good. One of my mentors, Professor Marion Edman, worked with Louise Rosenblatt in 1946 on an NCTE Intergroup Relations Committee. As Louise mentioned the work this committee did in her conversation with Mary, reflecting back on the history of multicultural education, a significant moment in my own learning came to mind.

I had a party when I became president of NCTE in 1979, which Marion and Louise both attended. They hadn't seen each other since that time more than thirty years earlier. They went off to a corner to reminisce about their struggles and accomplishments. Both recounted their rememberings to me a number of times after this encounter. They discussed the issues in the 1940s and the similarities of existing problems in the 1970s. They remembered their boycott of the hotel where they were meeting because African American committee members were barred from staying and eating at the hotel. Their boycott led to NCTE's policy regarding not meeting at segregated hotels. As I listened to their stories, reflected on the significance of these two women on my own work, I realized that I was a part of a dynamic history that informed me as a learner and a doer. I learned about the issues and struggles of democracy and cultural pluralism through my conversations with Louise over the years. My conversations took place not only in personal, face-to-face contexts, but in my long-distance discussions with their ideas through their writings.

My encounters with these women, and I might add with other women in this volume, enhanced my professional development. By hearing about their struggles, their failures as well as their successes, I could face my weaknesses as a professional, as a learner, as a contributor to professional education. I became confident that the struggles I worked through might result in some important advancement. We are all part of significant historical struggles in English education, and knowing that we are part of such a history helps us appreciate that the hard work we do is worth the energy we expend.

I hope that study groups in teacher education programs and schools in many places throughout the English-speaking world take the time to use these interviews as a basis for discussion and *action* and to open other conversations. Each conversation will help teachers explore the many questions they have, but will also help teachers understand that the answers are not in the statements of these professional teacher educators but in their own study and interactions with their peers as they respond *in active ways* to the comments and ideas of these outstanding women. Through such study, through debate, conversation, critique, analysis, talk, *we each can find ways to define ourselves as we tell our own professional and personal stories, as we make meaningful change in our teaching, and as we come to value who we are.* Thus we can learn to appreciate the language we use for reading and writing and our own learning potential.

Selected Bibliography for Yetta M. Goodman

I Never Read Such a Long Story Before. 1974. *English Journal, 63(8),* 65–71.

The Roots of Literacy. 1980. In *Claremont College Reading Conference: Forty-Fourth Yearbook,* edited by M. P. Douglass, 1–32. Claremont, Calif.: Claremont Reading Conference.

Kidwatching: Observing Children in the Classroom. In *Observing the Language Learner,* edited by A. Jaggar and M. T. Smith-Burke, 9–18. Newark, Del.: International Reading Association; Urbana, Ill.: National Council of Teachers of English.

To Err is Human: Learning about Language Processes by Analyzing Miscues (co-authored with K. S. Goodman). 1994. In *Theoretical Models and Processes of Reading,* edited by R. B. Ruddell, M. R. Ruddell, and H. Singer, 104–123. Newark, Del.: International Reading Association.

Reading Miscue Inventory: Alternative Procedures (co-authored with D. J. Watson and C. L. Burke). 1987. New York: Richard C. Owen.

Margaret Gill

My first conversation with Margaret Gill was at the fourth International Federation for the Teaching of English (IFTE) conference at Carleton University in May 1986. Margaret was one of the keynote speakers for the conference, whose theme was "Issues That Divide Us." I was moved by her opening address on empowering teachers and learners and dialoguing across communities. I remember boldly negotiating this interview on a sunny afternoon on one of the quadrangles of the Carleton campus. Margaret did not know me then, but her response to my interruption of her walk towards the Patterson building was friendly and enthusiastic. Our longer conversation, which follows, took place in a large, empty amphitheater on the Carleton campus on the last day of the conference while she and I waited for Margaret Meek Spencer to begin her keynote address on "Emergent Literacies."

Dialoguing Across and Within Communities

Empowering Teachers and Learners

MARY: Maybe you could begin by talking about the most memorable session you heard at this IFTE conference.

MARGARET: An important and recurring theme from many of the sessions I've attended centers on the questions: How do we give power to teachers? And how do we make sure we give power to our students? I've seen that issue tackled very dramatically and very usefully in a number of different ways. For example, Nan Elsasser and Pat Irvine, in their session on the ecology of literacy, talked about working with Caribbean students in a college in the Virgin Islands where the imported English language curriculum determines the acceptable forms of written discourse and the grading system. They described how, in encouraging the use of Creole to develop the students' sense of power in their mother tongue, they were then able to enhance the students' abilities in their "second language," that is, Standard English. The students come to college believing that they don't have a language: Creole is described, tellingly, as "broken English." Nan and Pat talked about the ways in which they have helped their students recognize that Creole is a real language, that they can write powerfully in it. The video examples of students reading their work were fascinating. The writing revealed different organizational and rhetorical elements, which led Nan and Pat to reexamine their narrow definition of the analytical essay in order to accommodate the discursive patterns of the literacy environment they were working in, and in which their students lived and would later work.

MARY: So you are saying that, when they write in Creole, they can handle the ideas from the real issues that produce real writing.

MARGARET: Yes, and the students hadn't previously been able to do that in their formally assigned college essays. So this example from the Virgin Islands, I think, is a memorable one because you can see a language that is seen as "inadequate," that is regarded as a deficit language, and you can see two teachers taking these students and their language and giving them the chance to write and learn in that language, to celebrate it, to see that it's as powerful a form of expression as, say, their music is. Yet the students' competence in Standard English also developed at the same time.

Nan and Pat ended their presentation with Freire's comment that "the fundamental theme of the Third World . . . is the conquest of its right to a voice, of the right to pronounce its word." So that is the first really thought-provoking session that comes to mind. But once I started to listen for this theme of how we give learners power, it started to turn up all over the place. In other words, this became the way I "heard" this conference.

MARY: What would be another example of a session in which this theme of empowering learners occurred?

MARGARET: Well, Donald Graves's presentation. I was set back a bit when one of the conference goers described Donald Graves as "that escapist Donald Graves," the suggestion being that he'd somehow opted out of the whole question of empowering students to become competent writers. I would want to disagree with that notion. It seems to me that what Donald Graves is arguing for is a classroom where children are allowed space in which to see themselves as writers; to define the areas of their life that they see as important to write about; to have responsibility for their writing when they draft, or tidy it up, or share it. This seems to me another example of empowerment in exactly the same way that Elsasser and Irvine's is.

In other words, Graves's elementary school children are not made to feel that their written language approximations are "broken English," but at the same time they are not deprived of access to the culturally dominant discursive forms of school writing either, any more than those Caribbean students are deprived of subsequent mastery of standard American analytical writing. There's been a distortion of Graves's work, I think. His "conference-based" classroom is much more than a model of the caricatured "child-centered" classroom. I think real empowerment is going on. So that's my second example. We can look at this pedagogy and see it as offering a way to construe young learners as having a sense of ownership of their learning, of their interpretation of their experience, and of the way it is put into words. In this sense it is a genuinely critical pedagogy because it has the potential to change power relationships in the classroom. I'd want to say that Donald Graves is political, not escapist. He belongs to an honorable tradition of radical educators.

As I sort of freewheel with this theme of power, it seems to me that we often turn the word *political* into something with a capital *P*, as if we can't do anything unless we change the system first: shoot administrators, or textbook committees, or whatever. But in fact we might do better to look at the term *political* as also referring to ways of working with the children in our classrooms in order to maximize their sense of membership in their own literacy communities, of what they can realistically do in their own world and in their own learning, and to examine the implications of this from a range of different perspectives. That would be a start.

For example, I'm at cross-decisions on the critique of literature as a form of moral technology. On the one hand, I read Terry Eagleton as saying that, really, literature teaches us to be sensitive and perceptive about nothing in particular; it encourages a seriously depoliticized subjectivity in the student. On the other hand, I was arrested by Gordon Pradl's talk, where he was arguing the role of literature as a powerful invitation to reflect on issues: seeing literature as encouraging a more hypothesis-testing attitude towards the world, one which celebrates human agency and choice. So I started to find that, even in the sessions that might have seemed to be disconnected from issues of power and learning, I still found the theme strongly there.

I move on again and I think about the sessions I went to on small-group learning. Here again, you have a highly political model of learning which can redefine the relationship in the classroom between teachers and students. Because once you change from a teacher-orchestrated, teacher-overseeing classroom model to one where small groups of learners are required to collaborate in deciding how they will achieve the required learning, you change the nature of the relationship between teacher and students. You change the nature of the relationship between one student and another. You also open up the classroom to the possibility of its being a place where other people might also come in, like parents, other adults, or even "remedial" people (to use that terrible word). I mean people who might work alongside the groups in your classroom. Once you've done this, you've done much more than simply move the desks around. You've invited the possibility of social patterns of learning that have the potential to be strongly empowering.

MARY: I think what you're getting at is really the sense of what children, any learners, can accomplish in a social environment.

MARGARET: That's right. The notion of helping students think for themselves seems such an innocent phrase, but as James Moffett said in the last session I went to, "If we really did the things we say we want to do, we'd scare the hell out of everyone, including ourselves." This means that the notion of seriously encouraging students to think for themselves would be another form of empowerment. So that's been one of the big things for me at this conference: listening to the suggestions of so many different teachers, researchers, and academics on the multitude of ways in which power might be more readily shifted to students in our classrooms to make them more autonomous, more efficient learners.

But also I've been paying attention to the theme of empowering teachers that's the other half of it! Sometimes, I think that when conferences focus on all the good things that in theory, or in an ideal world, teachers "ought" to do with their students, we have ended up making teachers feel pretty hopeless.

I think one of the other things we have to realize before we talk about empowering teachers is that it is the everyday demands involved in teachers' work that shape teachers' teaching choices. It's unreasonable to urge teacher change if that change is going to take up much more teacher time, if it's going to make teachers more tired, if it's going to make it seem hard to get on with colleagues in the staff room, or if it's going to make them have problems with the parents of the children they teach or the administrators who control their promotion prospects.

MARY: So that any notions of what we do for kids must take account of the extent to which the teacher feels empowered to take those ideas on board?

MARGARET: Yes. Again, in the teacher education session with James Moffett, we spent a lot of time talking about what is needed in order to give teachers the professional autonomy or confidence to do the things they may believe in, but feel they can't do—perhaps because they don't have the strength or energy, or even the ideological space to move in. And just to try and think this through for a minute: one possibility is that we should think more in terms of the small, everyday ways in which teachers can be supported in doing things they want to do, rather than in terms of the big things like international conferences and massive national projects. It might be more useful to consider little ways of supporting teachers' work in the classroom, like establishing informal networks amongst teachers so that they can meet from time to time, talk about what they're doing, get ideas from each other, and gain moral support. I think some of the classroom teachers

I have been talking with here have said that, for them, the really big thing about this conference hasn't been the big names at the top of the page. It's been the fact that they've sat with other teachers from other countries, from other provinces, and talked together about what made teaching hard, and what made it good, and what they could learn from each other. That, for them, has been the really big empowering experience from this conference.

Reflecting on Teaching, Researching, and Learning

MARY: I'd like to pick up on that. If we are going to empower teachers and really be nice about it, in what sense do you see them perhaps changing the role academia is currently playing in teacher education and practice?

MARGARET: Yes, I think we've got to go beyond the formal, empirical research models. And I think in a lot of countries in big and in small ways that's already happening, so that we are getting an alternative discourse initiated by people like Janet Emig. There are research models for quantifying, models from the experimental sciences. These are very useful, for example, if you want large-scale data: How much does it cost to keep a child in a government school for twelve years? What are the school retention rates for particular ethnic minority children? We need to know these things. But in very important areas such as how learning occurs—What's the relationship between language and learning? What's the nature of particular interactions between teachers and children in relation to learning?—we need a much more sophisticated research model. And it isn't a second-order research model, which I think is one of the dangers I see, when research is classified into first- and second-order categories of inquiry. The effect of putting an ethnographic research model, if you like, at the bottom and an empirical, quantifying model at the top, as Janet Emig points out, is to give the impression that the ethnographic model is a kind of second-order, warm, fuzzy, woolly research form.

MARY: Or mush-headed; and of course it isn't, as anyone knows who really engages in this kind of inquiry.

MARGARET: Yes, and we have researchers now to demonstrate that. Donald Graves is an obvious example. Shirley Brice Heath is an obvious example. Janet Emig herself is of course an obvious example. When we look at the way they operate and the results of their research, which can't be dismissed as warm, fuzzy, or mush-headed, then I think everyone, even the hard-headed quantifiers and the tough-guy behaviorists, has to sit back and start thinking about their own paradigms in terms of what *is* worth measuring or discovering, what questions are worth asking, and what are the research methodologies that will in fact generate reliable information and strong conclusions.

Now, it seems to me that what's very powerful about the research approaches that people like Shirley Brice Heath, Janet Emig, and Donald Graves have legitimized is the way they give power to teachers, the way they "use" teachers. They don't treat teachers, or their other research subjects, as research fodder; that is, the teachers are just there to constitute "data," to answer the researcher's questions, before the researcher disappears to publish the results in an important academic research journal.

MARY: You are saying then that teachers are the expert partners in this research enterprise.

MARGARET: Yes, so that in ethnographic studies the teacher's perception of the research is taken into account, the teacher has a role in generating and clarifying and making more relevant the researcher's questions, in working with the researcher to help the researcher see what is going on. Researchers cannot see it all; the teacher's interpretation of the ethnography of the classroom can strengthen the researcher's skills so that the researcher sees classroom events not just as "participant observer" (which is a weak term), but in a more intense and acute observer role. What is in fact happening then is that the researcher is having his or her research talents honed up by the teacher, and then you get researcher and teacher coming together to collaborate on the appropriate outcomes of that research. So what I'm wanting to say is that tough questions of how to improve classrooms and learning may be better answered by research models with a strong ethnographic base involving teacher and researcher and teacher *as* researcher.

MARY: What questions do you think in this particular conference we still need answers to? What issues do you think we haven't addressed? In other words, what are the questions that are worthy of pursuit? It seems to me that in a community of researchers, and researchers defined as you are defining them, both teacher and scholar or teacher, children, scholars—I would even take it that far—what are the things we don't know, we need to find out?

MARGARET: Sometimes we have the reaction that we need *more* information and *more* research, because there are problems in schools, and schools aren't as good as we want them to be. But look at all the things we know about English teaching and learning since Dartmouth. How come they're not happening?

MARY: We tend to have a reaction that we need more information, more research, and you think that we do not?

MARGARET: It's not a question of more information really. It's more a question of needing time for reflection, opportunity to come to grips with, or make operational, the good stuff we already know. One teacher said this morning, "It's not teaching well that's hard; it's getting into a position where you *can* teach well." I think that's often the case.

This leads to a consideration of what is the best kind of support which will help teachers have access to the best research or the best practice. I think there's a danger in all of this kind of talk that we create a deficit model of teaching—as if teachers aren't doing enough, and our job as teacher educators or researchers is to bring them the good stuff, the only question being, how do we get teachers to change and take it all on board. That's not quite what I want. My question is: How do we help teachers develop a reflective stance towards their own practice?

Teachers need time to stand back and reflect, "This was good. Why? I want to work on this." We don't give teachers enough time to just reflect. They dash from one class to the next. And if the class before generated important learning which they would like to nurture, they're into the next blackboard jungle before they have had time to think about how it happened. I think that creating an opportunity for teachers to reflect is one place to begin. As teacher educators that means developing in the students we teach their sense, as Schon would put it, of the teacher as reflective practitioner.

What's more, nobody wants to change, or even reflect on what they are doing if they have low self-esteem. You need to be pretty tough before you can go out and take on board someone else's ideas. To do that is to admit you're not perfect, that there are more things that you need to learn. I think it's that—that transition—helping a teacher have a chance to reflect on practice in a way that isn't threatening, helping a teacher see that making mistakes is not so terrible, which is our test mentality! What we should be doing is encouraging risk taking, and we've got to be able to see that that's a good thing to do. I'm having a disaster with a new undergraduate course I'm teaching for the first time this year. I spoke about it in my keynote address, and I'm trying to say to myself: This isn't really terrible failure with these students I'm teaching. This is me taking risks and I'm working on it.

The next question is: What *are* the grass-roots supports teachers need? This can often be the everyday things like the support of the school principal, or the way in which consultants can work with a principal and a department head, and not simply go straight at the teacher. It's important for teachers to feel that they've got at least a listening English department, rather than thinking of themselves as lone prophets. They need to feel that they can talk to their fellow members of staff, and critically so.

Here we need to think again about change to the institutional structure, so that schools become much more amenable to the support of adults from the community coming in, nonprofessionals who can be used as resource people alongside the students but also working with parents. This might result in freeing teachers up to feel that the school doesn't have to carry the whole weight of what it is to teach a student to learn, but that it's part of a visible partnership—and not just on parent-teacher night. If we could change the ways in which teachers can work with parents and their community, then I think that the "how do we get there?" question is likely to be answered. What we *do* when we get there isn't a problem, Mary: we come along to conferences and enjoy ourselves! But it's the question of the support teachers need, to help them recognize their own power and make sure they have more power, that I reckon is what we need to work on. I don't have a big research question in need of a big answer in there at all.

MARY: While we're talking about this notion of empowerment, why is it, for some people, such a scary concept? Why is it, at least as I see it from my vantage point in Canada, that empowerment is a very frightening concept to just the people that you are saying you want to work together: the principals, the teachers, the consultants, and the researchers?

MARGARET: Well, I think the idea I was trying to develop in my talk at the start of the conference was the idea that there are bigger forces in society at the moment that are taking away the appropriate autonomy teachers and principals should have, and therefore making them feel at risk. In the act of teaching, teachers need to feel that they have control over the decisions about what they teach and what is worth teaching; they need to feel they have control over the curriculum they are teaching; they need to feel they have control over the way in which their teaching is done and the forms of assessment which will enable them to evaluate their students' learning. What I worry about is the powerful profit-driven forces, like the testing industry and the textbook industry, which invade the areas that teachers rightfully control. When the prescription of textbooks moves outside the control of the teachers who have to use those textbooks, it takes away part of the teacher's ownership of her classroom and her ability to make judicious decisions in the best interests of the particular students in her class.

The imposition of mass testing can have a similar effect. If teachers are made to feel they have either been a success or failure, depending only on the basis of the scores that students get in national or state tests, then I think we are in deep trouble. I think it's understandable then if teachers don't want to take risks if, for example, they're in a school where the kids are doing really well on these tests and if the parents are happy with these glossy textbooks.

Teaching is a pretty fraught business. Part of you is always on the line all the time you are teaching children. There is often not much psychic energy left over to take risks. That is one good reason for the classroom model of small-group learning, which Moffett has been arguing for so eloquently this week. It is in fact a way of preserving the sanity and the energy of the teacher. In the long term, it takes pressure off the surveillance, the overseeing role. It redistributes the power and the control structures in the classroom.

MARY: I agree with you about teachers, but I'm wondering why empowerment is such a frightening concept to school board administrators and people at the other levels of the educational hierarchy?

MARGARET: I speculate here. Perhaps school board administrators have their own time-and-motion or cause-and-effect models of what they think accountability means. They have an assembly-line, industrial model of teaching, so that taking risks might seem to them like disrupting the assembly line or putting a spanner in the works. The machine might break down and the goods wouldn't be delivered at the other end. Presumably, the goods at the other end means little ticketed kids who can go straight into jobs with recognizable labels: employers can say, "Ah, yes I can see why I shouldn't employ him"; or tertiary institutions can say, "Ah yes, that student will fit." I think administrators probably feel they are at the interface between the demands of employers and tertiary institutions on the one side, and the needs of their students on the other. That's a pretty fraught interface. If you think about it, which group is bigger and has more power?

MARY: Which is why I asked my previous question about the role of the teacher. If we're going to really empower teachers, how can we change these structures, and the beliefs and the assumptions that come with some of these institutions?

MARGARET: I think that's why one would stress the importance of the relationship of teacher to principal, and of teacher-principal-staff to parents. But let's not forget that teachers and administrators are also parents. So maybe we should be asking for different definitions of possible relationships, and that's going to be slow. We heard some lovely examples this morning of schools doing just this.

MARY: Which ones do you have in mind?

Dialoguing across and within Communities

MARGARET: We heard examples of schools where the National Council of Teachers of English has recognized as Centers of Excellence schools which have changed the power relationships between teachers, principals, administrators, and school boards. The point was made that such institutional changes require confidence and trust. Interestingly these are human qualities, not necessarily pedagogical or professional ones. But time is needed before confidence and trust can have an outcome. Peter Medway, in his book *Finding a Language,* offers an example of how he wanted to develop a dynamic learning environment in his classroom. The sad end of that story was that his program lasted only two years because, at the end of that time, the parents were worried that the children wouldn't pass their "O level" exams, and the school principal withdrew his support. It failed partly because parent education and understanding were missing.

Some years back I was teaching in a secondary school. It was a very poor school, migrant children, mainly girls. The parents believed, appropriately, that because they were non-English speaking, what they wanted for their kids was very rigorous instruction in "good English" to get them jobs. We were about to change the prescribed English course book to one based on a seemingly freewheeling open curriculum which encouraged a radically different approach to writing development from the drills- and skills-based writing textbook previously in use. It didn't have any places for boxes for the right adverbial adjective to go in! It was designed on a much broader curriculum base, with room for child choice across a range of reading, writing, and oral language.

Before we brought the new program in, we had evenings with the parents to explain the change. I taught them an old-fashioned writing lesson with decontextualized grammar principles: short exercises, modal auxiliaries to put in the right place. That sort of thing. We got really bogged down with the shoulds, woulds, and oughts because of the difficulty of categorizing them from short sentences as presented in those terrible grammar books like your Warner's. And we worked away, and they were not getting very far, and also getting it wrong. Then I did another lesson with them, generating, talking, listening, reading, and writing, integrating language arts activities through exploring a particular issue they nominated. They looked at the way they had to talk about it, the way they had to research it, the thinking skills they needed in order to work on it, the choices of kinds of discourse they could use to write about it, the sorts of related reading that would be required—including reading what they'd written—and the kind of outcome which would enable them to evaluate the quality of what they had done. I asked: "In which of these situations do you think your children are going to be learning more English? In which do you think they'll develop better control and competence in writing and reading and speaking skills in English?" And no problems! We *can* let parents join in the dialogue; actually *come* into the classroom, and see it in action.

One unforeseen development in the school was in our approach to assessment. We used to have parents come in for parent-teacher night along with their kids as interpreters, because the parents' English wasn't strong enough. That in fact changed the way we handled assessment. Once you're feeding your evaluations of the kids' achievements to the parents, with the kids translating, you change your audience. You think, "What has the student learned that we can talk about together?" I think we learned as much as they did. We become better teachers when we begin to rethink this question of how we might help make schools become better places, and it was paying attention to the parents' expectations which helped us make improvements.

MARY: Picking up on that. Let's think about what Harold Rosen was getting at last night in terms of multiculturalism and "internationally there are few places in the world where we cannot think that multiculturalism does not exist," and think of Shirley Brice Heath's metaphor of teachers becoming more effective cultural brokers between home and community. How would you respond to this bringing of parents into the school, and teachers into the community? It seems more difficult to do.

MARGARET: Yes, I think it is difficult. For example, the Australian suburb in which I teach has seventy-five different cultural groups. There are large groups such as the Italian and Greek communities and, more recently, Chinese and Vietnamese communities. We have parents who are coping with massive cultural jumps themselves in getting jobs in a new country, handling a new language. Often at a very practical level, they're working daytime and nighttime shifts. The ideal notion of having them come in to the school and see what's going on or seeing the school as a community center isn't available; they're getting up to go to work when the kids get home. I think we have to have more flexible ways of going out into the community to talk to parents. In the situation that Harold described, the extremity of overt racism that his school faced meant that it welded teachers and parents into a community very quickly. Well, I wouldn't wish for that kind of terrible demonstration of racism as a way of accelerating a changed attitude for parents and teachers. I'd accept a slower pace.

We can recognize the cultural variety of families and accommodate them if we're sensitive enough. A nice example of that occurred in Melbourne, in one of the inner urban schools, with an NESB [non-English-speaking background] population of about 98 percent. The kids came from high-rise flats, tall buildings, with small rooms and no place to play. The local school had been really ramshackle: falling-down desks, chipped blackboards falling off the walls type of school. Then it got a federal grant, from a disadvantaged schools fund. I guess they exist in all countries. And so they built a marvelous open-plan school with the advice of some of our best elementary teachers with Gravesian commitments to writing, and plans for small-group learning and cross-age grouping and freedom for the children to move between different interest areas. Beautiful open planning. A lovely school! I'm working in it with my student teachers. It really looked great! But the little kids who came in from their tower blocks were absolutely disoriented by the space. They were used to a world of small spaces with walls close by which framed the ways in which they felt comfortable with other people. What that school did was to start ordering truckloads of temporary partitions and to construct smaller rooms, because they realized that they had to re-create small spaces in order to give these kids some sense of psychological security before they could socialize into the learning models that we had thought that they would immediately feel comfortable with.

MARY: One of the assumptions behind a conference is the bringing together of a community of people. Let's think back to Dartmouth for a moment and the interesting experience of the British and the Americans finding out at that conference that they didn't exactly see the world, or read the world, in the same way. From your experience of this conference in bringing the nations together, even the third world nations, do you think there are more issues that divide us, or are the issues at this conference perhaps ones that are uniting us more? What's your sense of where we're at?

MARGARET: My feeling, and right now it may be influenced by conference euphoria, is that, certainly in the sessions I attended, we have wanted to look more for consensus in the issues that seem to divide us. Where we've looked at major national concerns, it has produced more of an awareness that there are international political issues across countries which unite us. Also that within countries there is a diversity of conflicting issues.

I think I've valued the opportunity of meeting Canadian teachers. I've listened to the perspectives of teachers from Vancouver, Ottawa, and Montreal, and I've had a chance to begin to listen for the commonalties and differences in different communities of teachers. And of course because of Ian Pringle's policy for the conference of ensuring that participants were invited from all countries where English is taught or is an official or major language, I've had the opportunity to learn about countries that I probably will never have a chance to visit.

MARY: If I can just push you a little further, what would be your sense of the Canadian scene?

MARGARET: It seems to me that, like most countries, it has to be very mixed and that, depending on what province you're in, it's going to feel very different. I hold my breath at one point and think that the sun shines on Ontario and Quebec! and in the next breath that there are other parts of Canada that teachers feel are really bad news; where students are victims of mass testing; where teachers feel disempowered; where they are suffering impositions from above and where they lack either a sense of a national teacher union or the professional spirit to be able to shift these impositions.

That's a familiar feeling for me as an Australian, because we have states where the notion of teacher power, the notion of curriculum responsibility and assessment responsibility vary between total school-based ownership to centralized control by curriculum and exam boards. So I think what I've learned, as I did listening to two Nigerian speakers with differing perspectives about Nigerian education, is that Canada is like us. You have uneven examples of inspired practice, such as the really good practice I saw in a video by a Manitoba teacher. So I am sensitive and sympathetic to the notion that we always have these uneven distributions of what we see as excellence. And of course a conference like this brings us all together.

MARY: And maybe gives IFTE a better sense of mission of what it should be about?

MARGARET: Yes, I think that could be the case. The question arises: Can IFTE be much more than a mechanism that enables us to meet together every four years and occasionally disseminate good publications that have international value, like Jimmy Britton's book, our first IFTE publication. I think it's difficult for IFTE to see itself as having a role beyond that. Maybe one thing that's happened in Ottawa is a much more positive sense that IFTE does have something to offer not just to the tertiary jet setters or the professional researchers, but to classroom teachers as well. From an Australian perspective again, our policy was to encourage classroom teachers to come to Ottawa if they possibly could.

My feeling perhaps is that this IFTE conference has for the first time pushed the notion of IFTE towards being something that I think it ought to be, which is an international voice for classroom teachers. I think that's why I think you and CCTE and Ian need to be applauded, because my reading of history is that that hasn't happened before. Dartmouth was a most select body. York was an English occasion. Distance limited Northern Hemisphere teachers' access to Sydney. East Lansing was a limited occasion. This time, I think, we have had classroom teachers whose voices have been heard. Maybe not loudly enough, but they have been speaking in ways that I think are absolutely right. In our teacher education session this morning, we had a classroom teacher introduce a comment with "As a *practicing* teacher. . . ." The rest of us had become merely teacher educators—the marginal group!

MARY: You are returning to Australia. We all have our memories of a conference and, as you mentioned earlier in this interview, the euphoria of a good conference. What is the most memorable experience that you want to take back to your colleagues in Australia?

MARGARET: Well, this will bring the conversation full circle. The memory that's sitting in my imagination like a light, I guess, is Edward Kamau Braithwaite's poetry reading: his demonstration of the power of language when he told the story of himself as a poet, first through his early poetry with its European rhythms, to his growing recognition of his own Creole as in his present poetry, and its celebration (I can't say demonstration, I have to say celebration) of his language. When he read his poetry it was a politically powerful celebration of a language, a culture, and a society. So for me, and I imagine for a lot of others, that was a transforming moment and an inspiring one.

Teachers, Researchers, Learners

Mary invites us to "read and update." But eight years is a long time in education. IFTE's fourth international conference on the teaching of English at Ottawa is history. And though the issues raised in Ottawa are as relevant today as they were in 1986, they have now taken on a sharper focus, as the other interviews in this book make plain. Things need to be said differently. Things *are* different.

Take the word *empowerment,* for example. It now feels like a buzz word. Like the term *critical literacy,* it has come to suffer from overuse. It has lost its valency. I have made a private resolution to find a synonym. The term has been undermined from two very different directions. On the one hand, we have been overoptimistic in our belief in the "empowering" possibilities of democratic schooling and in our belief that schools alone can provide a socially critical curriculum which will "empower" students to participate more fully in society. "It is a very iffy thing, this schooling," as Rose (1989, 215) says in the book that more than most has influenced my post-Ottawa thinking.

"Empowerment" to participate more fully in society is not an automatic consequence of even the most effective critical pedagogy. It is equally the consequence of a broad and complex mix of factors: the learner's ethnic and cultural history, socioeconomic environment, personal qualities, genetic endowment, place, and even time. The Australia of the 90s (Henrietta Dombey charts a similar direction for the U.K.) is in the throes of massive economic and labor force restructuring. Unemployment rates are soaring; we are starting to talk about the permanently unemployed. We now know that, although teachers can work alongside their students in order to create conditions of *possibility* for empowerment, neither they nor any curriculum can guarantee empowerment in the world beyond school.

But the word is also undermined from another direction. Terms like *empowerment* and *critical* or *cultural* literacy, which initially carried such a charge for social reform, have now been not only qualified but tamed. They have been hijacked by conservative forces who have appropriated those words for their own agenda. The concepts have, as it were, been bought off and domesticated. Hirsch (1987), for example, in a book which appeared the year after the Ottawa conference, appropriates the term *cultural literacy* for profoundly reactionary purposes. He first argues uncontroversially that a competent reader must draw on socially contextualized cultural knowledge in order to read effectively (though Margaret Meek Spencer explains what this *really* means). But when he suggests that a schematic framework for skilled reading can be provided via a list of five thousand core facts which every American should know, he has misunderstood the nature of reading and trivialized the concepts of both culture and literacy. Culture can't be reduced to five thousand bits of factual information, or literacy to the passive possession of those bits. "Voodoo literacy" Scholes (1988) calls it. I thought I knew this in 1986. Social critics like Fairclough (1989) and Rose (1989) have taught me more.

Empowerment also turns up in revamped definitions of literacy, and there are problems here as well. International Literacy Year (ILY), 1990, provided the opportunity for yet another upgraded definition of literacy:

> Literacy involves the integration of listening, speaking, reading, writing, and critical thinking. It incorporates numeracy. It includes the cultural knowledge which enables a speaker, writer, or reader to recognize and use language appropriate to different social situations. For an advanced technological society such as Australia our goal must be an active literacy which allows people to use language to enhance their capacity to think, create, and question, which helps them to become more aware of the world and empowers them to participate more effectively in society. (International Literacy Secretariat 1990, 2)

So what? you might ask. It's a good definition. In Australia, ILY was responsible for another important initiative: the development of a major national policy statement by the federal government. *Australia's Language: The Australian Language and Literacy Policy* (1991) is a milestone. It concedes a culturally broader definition of literacy; it includes a policy for the maintenance of aboriginal languages; it expands programs for the learning of languages other than English. But alongside these policies it adds: "All Australians need to have effective literacy in English, not only for their personal benefit and welfare, but also for Australia to achieve its social and economic goals."

The familiar and reductive notion of "functional literacy" has returned in a new guise, revitalized in terms of the human capital needs of a postindustrial work force. Schools, once again, carry the burden for resolving a now heightened crisis in the economy. Schools are expected to make Australia, in the words of the prime minister, "the clever country." For "clever" read "internationally competitive." There is no prize for guessing who gets the blame when intractable international market forces fail to yield before the might of the little red schoolhouse.

It is in this context that Australia has taken the first steps to develop a series of National Curriculum Statements. They are not statutory documents with the same force as the U.K. National Curriculum, but they are designed to "guide" schools and curricula and to provide a framework for subsequent national testing, which so far in this country has been successfully resisted. In an attempt to provide an inclusive framework for English teaching, the first draft of the National Curriculum Statement for English appears to struggle. Standard English is affirmed as the main language of instruction in schools and as the "dominant" language in our culture. At the same time, the cultural diversity of Australian children is recognized. How are these principles to be brought into a fruitful relationship? The document cannot tell us.

Janet Emig talks about the value of holding a "hypothesis of commonalties" and points out that we have much to learn from recent cross-cultural studies in literacy, for example from the contrastive rhetoric studies of Kaplan. She also suggests we need to reconsider the "givenness" of the Western essayist tradition as the basic form for classroom writing, a discursive form which is not shared by many of the students who come to us. We need to allow differing ways of knowing alongside differing discourse patterns, a point which Elody Rathgen illustrates clearly in her account of the place of the Maori language in New Zealand's National Curriculum.

Can a National Curriculum accommodate these things? When certain knowledge forms are institutionalized, as in a National Curriculum, certain orientations are privileged over others. A dominant "ethnicity" is constructed. Any curriculum must be framed so that the struggle over its meaning and uses, that is, its ideology, can be explicitly and productively conducted. Where such explicitness does not occur, the message, as Patricia Symmonds warns, is a confused one. But it can be worse than that. It can lead to the oversimplifying of complex issues.

In Australia in recent years, there has been a narrowing in the debate over language and education. The implications of this at a time when a national curriculum policy is being developed are serious, particularly in relation to literacy pedagogy. Debate, for example, about the teaching of writing and genre theory has in recent years been dominated by one version of systemic linguistics deriving from the work of Michael Halliday. And while the usefulness of a Hallidayan approach to language analysis is not in question, the missionary zeal of the protagonists of one particular version of systemic linguistics has led to an unhelpful pedagogical polarization and a puzzling marginalization of the work of major sociolinguists, cultural critics, and cognitive scientists.

Looking back on my interview with Mary, I am still in agreement with myself on one point. I reflected in 1986 on the productive connection between language and learning, which Donald Graves's approach to the teaching of writing makes possible. I still think that is true. A year later, Giroux presented the same argument more cogently (Giroux 1987). Yet the critique of Graves's work in Australia has been mounted by systemic linguists in the narrowest of terms: "whole language," or Graves's "process-oriented" approach to the teaching of writing, is found wanting, framed in opposition to a "genre-based" pedagogy of the explicit instruction of the discursive rules of standard classroom writing. While this debate has had some value in energizing teachers' thinking and classroom practice, the cultural implications of Graves's work have been ignored.

The work of scholars across the broad fields of language, learning, and cultural studies must inform the development of national curriculum policy. Much can be learned from education systems in other countries and from international exchange. Rereading the interviews in this book reminds me how valuable and thought provoking such exchanges can be. So I am grateful to Mary for the opportunity to think—and think again.

Selected Bibliography for Margaret Gill

Who Framed English?: A Study of the Media's Role in Curriculum Change. 1991. Paper presented at the conference of the Australian Curriculum Studies Association, Adelaide.

The Teaching of English in Australia: The National Position Paper of the Australian Association for the Teaching of English (co-authored with others). 1987 (revised 1991). Canberra: Curriculum Corporation.

Preparation for Newspeak: The English Teacher's Responsibility? 1984. In *English Teaching: An International Exchange,* edited by J. Britton et al., 143–152. London: Heinemann Educational Books.

Three Teachers: Defining English in the Classroom. 1983. In *Timely Voices: English Teaching in the Eighties,* edited by R. Arnold, 78–95. Melbourne: Oxford University Press.

Politics and Power in Education. 1977. In *English in Teacher Education,* edited by M. Gill and W. Creeker. Armidale: University of New England Press; Melbourne: Oxford University Press.

Margaret Meek Spencer

I talked with Margaret Meek Spencer very late one autumn evening in October 1987 in her hotel room in Winnipeg, Manitoba. We both were invited speakers at the Manitoba Association of Teachers of English annual conference. I first met Margaret at Bedford College in London, England, the summer of 1982. She was an invited speaker for the English Teaching Institute organized by Stephen Tchudi. Margaret and I have had many conversations since, on both sides of the Atlantic. On each occasion I have come away inspired by and with full admiration for her perceptiveness and insights into people, contexts of situation, and what it means to be literate, which is constantly being redefined. Foremost on her mind in 1982, as at the IFTE conference in 1986, was expanding the definitions of literacy and literacy practices in home and school contexts. She continues that dialogue with herself and others in our conversation in Winnipeg.

Hesitations and Repetitions

The Practice of Literacy and Literacy Practices

MARY: For some years you have been concerned about literacy, schooling, and society in a general sense and, in particular, the literacy competencies that young children demonstrate before they are formally schooled in them.

MARGARET: Yes.

MARY: What do you see as the significant issues involved in the acquisition of literacy today?

MARGARET: I wish I could just number them off, one to ten, but that's not how it comes to me. Usually I'm reading something and what I'm reading suggests other things that other people have been saying about literacy. So it would go something like this. For a long time, reading has been separated too much from other forms of language, its uses and functions. Because there is a good historical reason for that, I've been probing a bit into the historical aspects of literacy to find out how people actually learned to read and write before the school made it something they had to do in a particular way. It becomes very clear that you have two aspects of reading and writing that we can't get away from. One of these is the whole social set up of the thing, the way it's socially ordered and demanded in terms of school. The other is the way by which people are valued, and those people who *are not* literate are counted as of less worth in society. What interests me is the way by which people come to regard literacy as something that everyone ought to have, even though they have no idea about what makes a person more literate or less literate. Once we begin to think of reading and writing in social contexts, then our view of teaching, learning, and literacy is bound to change.

MARY: What concerns you are the ways in which we assign value to literate behavior in particular social contexts and who decides on what counts as evidence of being literate.

MARGARET: Yes, that's one thing. The other thing that worries and interests me very much is the notion that, within the next ten years, the information technology revolution will certainly change literacy. Our ideas of it are bound to change. They've been changing for some time anyway. People's expectations of reading and writing will change. I predict that there will be big differences. Just exactly what these will be, I'm not very prophetic about, but already when we see banks of computers in schools, we know that pens, pencils, and books will be regarded differently. I don't mean that these traditional things will change any more radically for the better or the worse, but what *counts* as literacy will be different. It seems to me that now is a particularly interesting time to be looking backwards over how we came to be in our present situation, demanding more and more of literacy and, at the same time, creating new conditions where the old-fashioned reading and writing simply won't go on anymore.

MARY: What we expect of or demand of literacy will continue to influence the practice of reading and writing both in and out of school.

MARGARET: I think there's something else too. Throughout my life, especially since the war, people have believed that if education was better, however they determine *better,* then children would actually not suffer from the social and economic divisions which have played such a part in the lives of my parents and the parents of my contemporaries. That generation believed that somehow things would be better if there were better education and more of it. Now that we are faced with massive unemployment, there's a certain disillusionment, or at least disappointment, that for all our concern, we haven't actually brought about the paradise or the better land that we were looking for, and that education is not able to redeem us, not able to get us out of the situations that we're not too keen on. There are big questions and middle-sized questions and little questions about reading and writing that keep me going, I think.

MARY: What would be one of the bigger questions we have to tackle?

MARGARET: If it's about education, I think we've too often confined education within school—the notion that school will do the educating and that teachers will be responsible for better times or for doing certain things. The big question for us in England is this: What are people going to do with their time? We have so much unemployment and so many people are disillusioned about life. Education is bound up with important notions of work, and reading in particular has always been part of this. We've often thought that if you were good at reading, you would find a better job. We have to confront the relationship of literacy with people's notions of what they have to do and want to do. Now, I can't imagine there being a time when we won't have to help children learn to read and write. In fact, I'd be very sorry if we didn't, because for me the answer to the question "Why should they learn to do it?" is deceptively simple. I think it would be a great shame if children couldn't read a book or write one. But I don't think *we* actually know why *we* want *them* to do it; because if we were a bit clearer about that, we might find ways of helping the children to understand what's in it for them. The paradox and/or irony about reading is that there has never been so much available that's good to read and a lot of it being bought, and yet a great deal of belief that people don't do very much reading and writing. I think they do much more than we think, and they're better at reading and writing than we know. I want to know *what* relates the way we teach reading and writing to the kind of roles these things play in people's lives.

MARY: We need to think about how we can engage teachers and children authentically in these interpretative social practices.

MARGARET: Yes, and in this changing world no single definition of literacy will serve us.

MARY: If the reality, the present condition, is that we still have teachers and children who come together in institutions, in schools which define how literacy *should* unfold, how do you see a group of teachers and children regaining a sense of hope, a more meaningful role for literacy-literacies in their daily living?

MARGARET: The first thing we do as teachers is to abandon the notion that somehow we have to be accountable to politicians. Somehow teachers have to be freed from the need to produce test scores of the kind that are actually used against them and their children as evidence of reading failure. Once teachers get hold of the idea that there is nothing different about learning to read than learning other things, then I think it may help them to teach children all the better. Teachers who work with us in reading projects are also actively teaching children to read. We suggest that the secondary school teachers learn to teach primary school children and the primary school teachers go to secondary schools. The first thing we discover is that they can do that. The second thing we discover is that they ought to be speaking to each other much more about what they do. I don't know whether that has anything to do with reading or not, but it certainly has a great deal to do with teaching and learning. When teachers do this, they bring back to the class the kind of evidence that is rarely allowed into studies of reading. I say "allowed" because we've taken it so much for granted that we never thought to look at the things that we see all the time. So, I'm not unhopeful. In fact, I think that teachers at this moment are absolutely splendid. They're often better trained than they've ever been before; they're learning how to get rid of the shackles of a kind of totalitarianism about method which is binding them down, and they have good ideas. They mind about children's learning and understand it very well. And they read the key books and consequently are far more enlightened than I was twenty years ago. I have no doubt about that.

MARY: Speaking of key books, I notice that you are reading James Wertsch's book, *Communication, Culture and Cognition: Vygotskian Perspectives.* One of the arguments Vygotsky makes is that it's the school's responsibility to develop the child's highest potential. How do you see teachers dealing with his notions of development and learning?

MARGARET: Well, let's leave the notion of development on one side for a moment and think of the things in Vygotsky that teachers rejoice about when they learn them and experience them. The first one is about language being a social act. That sounds so obvious, but I think that's a great breakthrough for some teachers. The second thing is that when you read Vygotsky, you feel that you're in a great encounter with a genius. Bruner says he's one of the great titans of the century, and I think he's right. Once you learn to detach Vygotsky from the earlier Pavlovian idea of stimulus and response, then you find that his concern about instruction is not just a notion that someone will tell children after all; that is, there is only a proximal development if not just a blank space that teachers have to fill. When Vygotsky talks about instruction, doesn't he include other, more experienced peers as well as adults? The zone of proximal development has been variously interpreted, but the constant is his notion of the more reflective persons lending their conscious grasp to the less experienced.

MARY: Yes, we have a long tradition in schooling of teachers perceiving their role as one of readying or preparing children for literacy, reading or writing. This readiness notion is even found in recent studies of "collaborative learning," in which the teacher prepares children for collaboration by modeling behavior or providing routines and formats for working together. In most instances, I think they haven't really understood why they want children to work together or fully understood what Vygotsky meant by children learning and playing as social practice in a social context.

Play as Concept and Play as Experience

MARGARET: Yes, and another thing is that we need to learn a lot more about Vygotsky's notion of language as a tool and that business about the second signal system. The second signal system is the world encoded in language. Once we've got the hang of that, I think it goes from there. The bit I like best, of course, is about play. Every teacher can understand that play begins at the moment when the child has unrealizable desires and that play is really serious business. Once you've got the hang of what he's all about when he's talking about the pivot thing—the stick and the horse—then the metaphor becomes the most exciting and wonderful analogy about language and language use. We pay too little attention to this, probably because we are so aware of the fact that language is functional. It is also something that children play with and get a lot of understanding out of language play. One of the greatest discoveries for a child is that a sentence can say what *is,* as well as what *is not* the case. Once a child has discovered that, I think language becomes a very powerful tool. Teachers respond to that idea with enormous gratitude because they see that what they're dealing with every day of the week is exactly where all learning is concentrated.

MARY: Would you elaborate more on this notion of play. What might this mean in written language development and the whole notion that Vygotsky talks about of children making transitions from oral to written language?

MARGARET: Let's consider the early years of children's writing and drawing. I think we need to look much more into that kind of symbol making before we realize exactly what the system—what the process—is. Consider the notion of tool use and early writing. Children do it with a tool, and the whole way by which those marks become meaningful symbols needs to be explored. I think there is, on the one hand, a kind of a vulgar behaviorism which suggests that if children do enough copying, they'll get better at writing. On the other hand, there are a lot of high-flown statements about writing which don't connect easily for teachers with what the kids are actually doing. The teachers who take on Vygotsky's notions of play and tool and try to see what they can report from what they see (because after all they must have much more evidence than anyone else) are in an informing position. Their evidence should count, and they make sure that it does.

MARY: Yes, I certainly agree. How would you respond to some teachers who say, "Well, play is fine, but I'm teaching in the middle grades. That's not a time for play; they must get into serious business"? I recall one grade 2 teacher putting it this way, "This kid is in grade 2 and doesn't have time to waste playing."

MARGARET: Yes, that's the kind of thing people say who have the exams in mind. They have already counted the years and believe that children should get a move on. I'd rather we didn't keep reminding ourselves of what we ought to do all the time. The thing which Vygotsky taught me was that when you were actually working with something in play, there came a moment when you actually stopped playing and began to notice the nature of the thing you played with. I think that that's more true of language than anything else. Problem solving seems to me to be a very refined kind of play. What we need to teach teachers to do is to stop talking about "just play" as if play were some kind of inferior form of behavior that you grow out of. This is the same with storytelling, the same with narrative. Teachers say they observe that children tell stories, lots of lovely stories, but they have to get down to learning how to write that serious essay.

MARY: Some believe exposition to be a more complex genre than narrative.

MARGARET: Yes, children are urged to give up imagination and become "scientific," to sequence prose, and present it in logical order and do all that essayist tradition I've been schooled in. I think that these things are very serious. But I also think that narrative is more than just narrative. It seems to me that its varieties of structures are learned very early on. Certainly all those things in Proust's childhood are very much a part of all of that and are reflected in his classic novel, *Remembrance of Things Past.*

MARY: That whole novel is just a playful activity on ideas.

MARGARET: It's very beautifully structured, very subtle. I discovered late what a good comic novel it is, and therefore all the more serious as social criticism. Far, far more than that, it's the best research we have on memory and feelings. Children are very percipient, and when we think they're playing, they're trying out a whole view of the world. They actually learn much more about possibilities than adults do. Adults settle for less than children do. If we keep on insisting that children must settle for less, round about the ages of seven and eight that's when we focus in on them, we get less. We need to stop underestimating what children can do and what they tacitly know. To digress for a moment, I had a very exciting time today reading the accounts of Nicholas Polanyi's response to his Nobel Prize, and reading all the things that he did to get it, and remembering that every single thing that he was saying has its echo in that book by his father about *Personal Knowledge*. It seems to me, here is someone who knows, who plays at what he's doing as a child does with his father's ideas.

MARY: The great thinkers of this decade have been the people who have allowed their ideas to take them into other worlds.

MARGARET: It may be that. But I think if you look at them, they all took play pretty seriously—Bruner and Polanyi and certainly Vygotsky, who undoubtedly did see that, at the beginning of the Revolution, everything was possible. But what school does, and this is what worries me about the present situation in the school, is that it narrows down a lot of things that would have remained as potential if we hadn't used the authority of school to *school* it. We've done it in the way that we school horses, by making them perform actions that we want them to perform, rather than the action that they would, if left to themselves, actually perform. I don't mean that we should leave them all to run wild, because that's irresponsible in other ways.

MARY: You see us as needing to put more faith in the tacit tradition and the possible.

MARGARET: Well, I think we need to do that. But we also need to let childhood and children be more free. It's the only way to excuse the fact that we keep them children for a long time. There is no point keeping them out of the adult status for a long time if we don't make the most of that period *for* them, and *with* them. If we simply expect early adult behavior of them without giving them adult responsibility, I think that's a pity. I like the view of reading that you apprentice yourself to someone to learn what the master is good at. What good engagers of apprentices used to do was to mediate the task to the younger persons, while at the same time making them responsible for that bit of the task. The problem came of course when the apprentice did it better than the master. In one Scottish legend, the mason wanted to carve classic pillars and his apprentice wanted to carve gothic ones. The master threw the hammer at the apprentice's head. Well, I see a lot of us throwing hammers at children's heads and, consequently, their natural inventiveness is too early cast down.

MARY: How do you see us reversing this whole notion of the school arresting children's potential, natural curiosity, and inventiveness through play?

MARGARET: I don't think all schools do it. I just think that we are falling into the trap of thinking that accountability accounts for everything. I'm not even suggesting that children should never be subjected to any form of assessment, but we must assess them in such a way that we stop making it an individual thing. The other possibility would be to try to devise ways of learning in school which make the most of the nature of school as a social institution. I ask why we don't make all the creativity of the young into something we are glad about. We can do the same with teachers.

Let me tell you about the treatise I've been working on. From time to time, I become very impressed by teachers' intuitions; the kind of things they know about, say a child's difficulties or why one class can't get on with it and another class can. These are the kinds of things teachers have always known, really, but when you look at the educational research, you seldom find reference to that because on the whole teachers themselves would describe it with their usual tentativeness as "hunch" or "anecdote." They're always terribly afraid that they'll be put down, because they tell people things in a way which they think scientists would say was *just* anecdote. But once we begin to dignify anecdote and, in particular, teacher anecdote and give it its place as narrative, we begin to notice that teachers trust these hunches. We did it ourselves, for example, when we were trying to find out why some adolescent boys couldn't read.

We have totally failed to ask children what they think reading is, because we don't think that their responses will be evidence. These will just be childish views of reading. But as their view of the task is the one which is ordering the way they do it, then it just seemed to me a good idea to start asking children what they thought reading was.

Learning in the Potential and the Potential in Learning

MARY: That would also, I think, probably extend to their whole view of literacy as well. I'm reminded of Sue Ervin Tripp's comment that children have frequently been observed by ethnographers, but they've been seldom interviewed about what they think about language. Halliday says something similar when he talks about teachers needing to know more than just about language. They need to understand what children perceive language to be.

MARGARET: Absolutely, and it's interesting that when I was looking at Shirley Brice Heath's work with my students last week, I had also been re-reading Halliday's *Language as Social Semiotic.* A lot of the things that she's saying, he was actually into in 1978; for example, saying that learning to read is learning the culture. So I think, and I should have said this at the beginning, that we need more cultural studies, really good ones. And also we need to understand that the ethnographic procedures have a theoretical background which is implicit in the way we go about inquiry.

MARY: Yes. Let's go back a bit to your comment about cultural studies. I agree with you in terms of the need for more of them. Do you see any dangers in terms of who does the cultural studies and how they get done and who reports the results?

MARGARET: Oh yes. I'm thinking of the kind of stereotype of the anthropologist going into a strange country and making assumptions about the natives that are not necessarily the way in which the natives would be or see it. And it comes back to your whole notion you were talking about earlier, this whole notion of authenticity and young children—that they really do see the reality of things, even in their play.

MARY: How do you see this relating to what teachers and children do in school?

MARGARET: This year we've done some things with teachers which have put writings like autobiographies at the center of things. It's in the second course of the master's program, which Jane Miller and Tony Burgess do. They introduced me to a book called *In Search of a Past* by Ronald Fraser, a man who wrote a very impressive book about the Spanish Civil War. As a child he had lived in a mansion in the tradition of the English upper middle classes. At a critical period in his adult life, he discovered that he could not recollect any details of his early childhood. While undergoing analysis, he interviewed the servants. Here's the crucial point. When Fraser was young, no one asked the servants about anything; their opinions—and they had many. Later, their recollections were revelatory. You can imagine that aunts', uncles', and cousins', and schoolmasters' reports were all part of the biography; all this evidence was lying around. But the richness of what he got was from the servants just by taking a tape of their comments and asking what it was like when they worked and how they saw him and his parents and so on. He suddenly discovered a whole world that he actually inhabited and about which he thought he knew absolutely nothing. And as they caught on to little pieces, he remembered being involved. He got a much more complex view of his past, and, of course, he puts it together in a different way too. There's that one, and then there is Carolyn Steedman's autobiographical study of her mother in the book called *Landscape for a Good Woman.* (You remember, she wrote *The Tidy House,* about children writing. That's the kind of study I think we should be doing.) In writing about her mother, she is also writing about her life with her mother, right up to her mother's death. It's a very painful book because what hangs over it is the fact that she discovers she's illegitimate, accepts it, and copes with it, but at the same time, she understands that for her mother this was a terrible situation which she was dealing with all the time Carolyn was young. Everyone has that story; I don't mean the same story, but we all have, as it were, our own history within the culture which we inhabit.

MARY: Let's relate this to one of our earlier themes, the constraints of the school system on literacy and emergent literacies. How do you see this writing of autobiographies in school operating in cultures in which the trust in the school system is precarious? For example, many of the recent ethnographic cross-cultural studies demonstrate discontinuities between home and school.

MARGARET: Two things come to mind. The first was the day before yesterday, when I was talking with the high school teachers (in Winnipeg). They were telling me about the native students in their classes in the inner city, who never said anything, who always were silent, and whose habit it was to sit and let everyone else talk. They discovered that on the whole this is part of a pattern which actually exists outside school as well as in school. They could have been forgiven for thinking that the school was silencing these students. But in fact, silence is a form of respect for your elders, where you don't initiate the questions and you don't speak unless you're spoken to. That behavior of the native students is maybe part of a cultural pattern which the school doesn't know about.

Learning the Rules of Discourse: Possibilities and Expectations

MARY: This points out how little we know about the lives of students and how many suppositions and assumptions teachers have about them. Susan Philips demonstrates this very well in her book about native students on the Warm Springs reservation, *The Invisible Culture.*

MARGARET: This is particularly true in England, where middle-class teachers think they know about working-class children, when in fact they have very little idea about them. The assumption of the easy sliding over from home to school always has to be looked at in specific contexts. But it's more than that. While I was reading Shirley Brice Heath's book, *Ways With Words,* what I was asking myself all the time was: Why did the children of Tracton have to conform to the main town school patterns? I know that she thought it would be better if the teachers understood about the nature of the literacy events in the lives of these children, the nature of the narrative traditions, the ways in which they learn to tell stories and to talk. I kept thinking that there was never any doubt that these children had to conform to what went on in the school. I had that feeling, you see, that even when the teachers understood all this, there wasn't going to be any way in which these children would be let off conforming to the main town pattern. And that's always bothered me. Because what we've discovered in London is that, if we don't silence minority groups, they can do just as well as any other group of children the things the school wants them to do.

This having to conform to the school's way of doing also shows up in Sarah Michaels's study of sharing time among black and white students' storytelling patterns. She makes it very clear that the storytelling habits of the black children are different, but the teacher was always cutting some children down to size, to what she wanted for classroom display. If we encouraged children to do what they were already good at, we would actually get more than we expect. I see that all the time in school, with the way we're looking at transitions from home to school or one school to the next. Children are inhibited not because they can't do things, not because they're afraid of the teacher, but because they're looking all the time to find out what the discourse rules are. They're making sure that they conform first of all to the discourse rules, and they've learned to do that very well by the time they are about seven or eight. We should also be more aware of the way by which we actually create the discourse rules of the classroom. You know, the "How do we do things around here" is what they're always looking for. The children who have least difficulty are those who know how to conform, and those who don't conform get shut out. So it's not only that we need to know about culture. We need to know more about what children are capable of.

MARY: Do you see this conforming to the discourse rules of a school or classroom applying to how children go about reading and writing in school and getting on in life?

MARGARET: Yes, very much so and what counts as evidence of being good at it. What was so wonderful for me with respect to this issue of literacy competency was the beginning of the whole-language and psycholinguistic movement and the suggestion that you did the thing *for real* from the very start. It wasn't that you practiced from any old scrap, anymore than these people who learn only to play scales may become terrific technicians. But it's the interpretation that sorts out the good players from the poor players, that is, the ones that do it with their head and their feelings as well as their fingers. I know plenty of people who read terribly well but it doesn't mean anything; you know they're not with it. I think it's not the beginners that I worry about, it's the ones who have to move off their first understanding of what you have to do, to doing what readers do. I want kids to do what readers do from the start—whatever it is that readers do. I think those who are apprenticed to readers have the best chance.

But I also want someone to watch children who do not have bookish parents, to see what they really do in response to their reading lessons. Observing the bookish child with the bookish parents is an important step in the business; we've learned a lot about reading from these children. But I want to know how the native North American comes to terms with a book which is not part of that culture, and why the Caribbean child in England cannot read without feeling that the teacher is condescending. The Scottish child has always had a lot of help because there is a very old tradition that reading is what you learn to do—it's what you go to school to do. But I don't think they are very much further forward than they were a long time ago. I think the teachers have the evidence. But the real key is how we can collect it sensibly and authentically.

MARY: Do you think that the universities have much more of a responsibility in legitimizing this collecting of evidence from the teachers' point of view than they have thus far assumed?

MARGARET: Let's come at this slightly differently. At one end, English departments in universities select only very good readers for their students. They have proved themselves by examinations, by the accountability, by the tests, by the subtlety of their responses, by the impeccability of their prose. Then professors set them reading exercises for four years; they do literary criticism, a very sophisticated form of reading. And at the other end, we have all those studies of children beginning to learn to read. But where would you look for an account of how a really expert reader is made? Do you know one of those? I don't know one.

At each stage, we separate readers and writers fictitiously from knowers and doers by acts of administration. For instance, we tell the chemists that they don't have to do any more reading of narrative; we tell the physicists that they have to read only physics books now. And then everyone gets a little push in the reading specialty of his or her text area. We give sixteen- to nineteen-year-olds highly specialized instruction on information retrieval, which I just call reading. And then we look at computers—and they all have to be read—the whole complicated thing goes on. But no one makes the process clear at both ends, let alone in the middle. At the beginning, what kids do is clearer than it was; at the other end of, say, something like reader-response, but between that—the beginning and the end—what do teachers know about good and bad readers? They just assess them as good or bad or good and less good or competent and less competent, but nowhere do we look at the way by which it happens. We assume that those who have most competencies are those who have read most kinds of texts *and know they can.* They have a grasp of consciousness of what they're up to.

MARY: Well, how conscious should this awareness of what they're up to be?

MARGARET: The thing which intrigues me is that if you want to read a modern novel, you don't first have to take a course on how to read older literature like *Tristram Shandy* before you start. You don't say, "Right. I'd now like to read *The Handmaid's Tale,* so I'd better have some warm-up exercises." You don't do this; you warm up on the first five pages. You assume that the mastery you have already can be stretched to something which you have never encountered before. Now this must be going on through children's life in reading all the way through school. There are those young readers who tolerate the uncertainty of whether or not they'll be able to do it, and those who stick at the sweet-dreams level or the newspaper level—if it's levels? I don't think it's levels; I think it's discourse kinds. What we could argue is that children in school learn different discourse kinds. And that's what schoolteachers teach—the geography book, the history book, the science book, or the writing of the report, the writing of the narrative, the writing of the short story—that's what we're actually up to. The ones who seem to have the most mastery are the ones who have most experience of most kinds. And you can see that's the case if you look at children who have remedial reading lessons. They mostly get very little. They're always doing less of the total and more of what they can't do. That's what's wrong with remedial reading lessons. Maybe we have to look for ways of making these children grasp the nature of the task better, without it being a teacher's description of the necessary operations to fulfill the teacher's requirements and expectations. Does any of that make sense? You see, because you're asking me, I'm thinking about what we do to make children good at reading. I'm not sure, but what always worries me is that people who don't write teach writing, and people who don't read teach reading. It does seem a bit loony if you were to invite a non-piano player teacher to teach your child to play the piano.

MARY: What about the teaching of literature?

MARGARET: We should begin to talk about that from another way in. Remember Ian Reid's notion of literature. He has two models. He says in literature we always operate on the museum model where we take out "the piece" and actually annotate it and write the ticket and keep it inside the glass case. But if we had a workshop model of reading and writing, then I think that what you would have to do in the workshop is to read and write. So that, as James Britton suggests, a ten-year-old who decides to write a novel can be apprenticed to a novelist. The relation of reading and writing is the missing part of this discussion so far.

MARY: So what you are saying is that really, in terms of mastering the conventions, whatever those conventions are, whether it's the conventions of doing school or a discourse, you would like to see more of a playing with the conventions.

MARGARET: Yes, just having a go at it. This means not just following rules but making the rules.

MARY: You don't believe in recipes to learning, linear steps models of "This is the way you do it," which leads to the view that "If I follow these steps, I can do such and such."

MARGARET: Right. I think of Tennyson's comment, "Lest one good custom should corrupt the world." When people try to imitate the process model of writing, I think of what Don Graves did in classrooms and what people try to make children do. "If only we could be Graves" or "I'm doing the Graves method." Don of course would not subscribe to this.

I'll give you a nice story which I like very much. When I was in Bath Boys' High School, in my early days of watching teachers learning to teach, I went to the assembly, which used to begin every English school day. This school had a very mad headmaster, who would suddenly stop everything to ask questions to make sure the boys were paying attention. This particular day, the passage was from Acts in the New Testament, the story of the Abyssinian eunuch reading in his chariot. Philip goes up to him and asks, "Understandest thou what thou readest?" The headmaster suddenly shouted out, "Stop." The prefect, who was reading, stopped and the headmaster said loudly, "We have a visitor from the university today who is going to go around to discover how you understand what you read." Then he went on at length expounding the necessity always to understand what you read. Towards the end of this interruption, his voice rose to a great climax, and he shouted, "What I'd like from this school is for you all to be Abyssinian eunuchs." There was a certain amount of horrified silence, and somehow we got back from the hall to the classroom without laughing. But the question "Understandest thou what thou readest?" has stuck with me since that day. My answer is quite often, "No I don't. I only half get it." It was I. A. Richards who wrote a nice piece about how to read a page. He said, "When you read something you can't read, read it as if it made sense and perhaps it will."

MARY: What about writing?

MARGARET: Oh, I'm the last person to give lessons on writing. You see, I write everything about sixty times. I don't compose on a word processor because I find I can actually rub it out faster than I can cancel it on a machine. I adore writing because it's like a romantic agony. I think it's that for me. I think it's the only way I understand what I'm thinking. But the real excitement lies in a particular kind of discovery, a revelation that I know, understand, grasp but can't explain. So I'm very bad at it. I want the text to be, in the end, as if it were effortless and it's just a terrible effort.

MARY: Do you agree with Vygotsky that it's a higher, more complex form of language?

MARGARET: I think it's just one more abstraction, without making it higher and more complex, you know, than it really is. Some actually suggest that it's what separates the sheep from the goats in literacy.

MARY: Is that because we have such a tradition of thinking this way and because that's the most conventional way in which we evaluate?

MARGARET: Yes, I don't understand why the essay has become such a kind of marble form. We actually teach writing as if it were chipping words in stone and as if they had to last forever. I think the important thing for children to learn is that there can be change, and to be satisfied with the interim. You can still throw it away and do it again. But on the other hand, it does stay, that's the point, isn't it? That's the good thing about it. I'm hopeless in talking to you about writing. I just do a lot, think it's important, and spent all my childhood being told I couldn't do it. I think perversity made me stick at it. I never thought I'd see anything of mine in print. I think people should write more verse than they do, very satisfying stuff that they can wrestle with. People just need to do it. I do it every day, in case one day I should wake up and find I can't do it at all. It's like playing a stringed instrument: you can't not practice, at least for me. But lots of other people do. I know James Britton walks up and down, and then sits down and writes something perfectly. He's a Mozart. I have to converse on the page; I'm a Beethoven rather than a Mozart. But Beethoven composed, however, without any changes when writing songs because the words held the form for him.

MARY: We've come full circle in this interview; we started off with the themes of literacy, schooling, and society, and you've just told me a lovely story about your own perceptions of yourself as a writer. What do you like to say to teachers who teach writing and who don't write.

MARGARET: I think teachers just don't write because they're afraid of not being able to do it. And they're always teaching writers who can do it better than they can. I read enough of my students' work to know that they're much better at it than I am. I'm disinclined to give teachers advice because I don't want them to rest on anyone else's wisdom. I really don't want them to take my word for anything. I would rather they were highly skeptical of anything that any would-be guru tells them. I could change my mind about this next week. I don't know anything that teachers and students haven't taught me. The wisdom comes from working on something with other people, so that you have something between you that you can look at and share. You know what you do in your class when you bring in tape recordings, and two people look at them: they begin to reflect things that neither one of you could have discovered on your own. The fact that you're both looking at them gives them a different kind of validity. You're not solely responsible for the judgment.

Now, I want to find out ways in which teachers can collaborate with their pupils and their students so that being a pupil or a student is not a subsidiary role; it's a learning role and a teaching role. It's a partnership. I know that I have to learn how to help my students to learn. Unless I do that, I might as well stay at home. If I think I have a recipe package, why don't I just put it on a tape recorder. Then we can all stay at home and needn't come to class. But it's the way in which a class or a group works that is for me the exciting teaching and learning situation.

MARY: What you're saying is that the school should not be conceived as a school as we know it but as a learning community.

MARGARET: Quite, and whether in fact it conceives itself as that, it is that. Sometimes what you learn is that "life is grim, life is earnest, but the grave isn't its goal." For teachers and students the line should have been, "And the *grade* is not its goal." The child and the student do not have to be diminished in any way, nor does the teacher. Our hierarchical educational system is actually based on the form of diminishing the ones who are less good at learning in the school's terms. The minute we stop learning from teachers and children, then I think we should just give up, because we certainly won't be of any use to either of them.

MARY: On that note, is there anything else you would like to say?

MARGARET: Well, thank you. I don't know. Maybe. When I was writing about reading in *Learning to Read,* I thought one day, "This won't do the job I wanted it to do, because it's me at a distance." So I wrote what I think is the best line in the book: "If you don't get your questions answered by reading this book, write to me care of the publishers." I didn't think anyone would take that seriously, but they did. I got hundreds of letters. The most interesting thing about them was that they began by saying it was a great thing to read the book because it made them feel better about what they could do with their children. This meant that I was satisfied because I hoped that's what would happen. They then went on to tell me how they read with their children and what they'd been doing, and they really wanted me to write back and say that that was all right. And clearly from what the writers were saying, they had a great time and they'd also—even when they thought they weren't doing it very well—discovered something about the process of reading the text and thinking about it. The most intriguing thing for me was that no two letters were the same, all these people describing what they did with their kids. This has totally confirmed my belief that if you want to do anything, you can do it, but it's the wanting to that is the interesting thing. I don't think we know enough about that, but Vygotsky, I think, got it. That is, between the bit that you can do and the bit that you want to be able to do is not a black hole, but it's like crossing stepping stones on a fairly fast-flowing river. You don't absolutely have to have hands held out to you, but it's good to know they're there. So it doesn't really matter what I think about reading; people will go on reading just the same.

Later Reflections

The conversations in this book derive their significance from the fact that they are not what Julia Kristeva calls "bounded text." Instead, they are continuing, fluid dialogues, over time, weaving in and out of each other, held by the imaginative skill of the editor. Mary Maguire asks, listens, and then nudges. The discourses flow and ebb. This is the spacious kind of recursive talk that helps thinking, unusual now in cultures of snappy, modish sound bytes, where time is money. The topics overlap, advance, recur, like movements of the sea. You must have noticed in your reading of these pages how the leading questions to the speakers release more ideas and awarenesses than the speakers themselves had perhaps bargained for at the outset.

Some encounters are more neatly ordered than others. Each is located in the particular place and time of its occurrence. Most of us were passing through Canada, which, as we spoke, was high in our conscious awareness of sameness and difference, especially when we discussed teaching and learning. For all of us I guess, Canada has always been a place of preeminently warm hospitality, not least to ideas, and of generous giving, not least of intellectual foodstuff.

Although we now read these conversations in a book, each dialogue still attests the primacy of speech, the expressive force of "language close to the self" that James Britton emphasizes and taught us to care about. In our different teaching roles and locations, we all hold to a common notion that "language, when it *means,* is somebody talking to somebody else, even when that someone else is one's own inner addressee." Revisiting these encounters, I tune the pages with the voices of the speakers. At the same time, I am stirring up and pushing on my own reflections as they have grown and changed since that late night in Winnipeg in October 1987, a time when, in England, we teachers knew we were about to face what we feared.

Above the recurrent themes, common concerns, and individual viewpoints, there rises a strong sense of this book as a collaborative enterprise, something we could not have fully experienced in the interview. We are each now part of something that both confirms and extends our thinking and, at the same time, problematizes it for us. "Did I really say that?" English is our common language; our involvement with it is central to our professional lives. Our confident use of it we take for granted, yet each of us inhabits a historical and social nexus implicit in what we say and how we say it. Mary underlines this from time to time, so there is no mistaking the different voices and the many-stranded traditions. We also show an awareness of our parochialisms and of how the standard language which supports our discussions also inhibits our students. We have all lived through, in our different cultures, nearly half a century of social and educational change. So, as we talk about our professional preoccupations, you must have found some ideas that you might have expected to divide us, and they don't, and others that we might have taken for granted as the same are different. What follows now is, from one of the oldest and certainly not the least voluble talker, some thoughts about these ideas, written this time, in tribute to my colleagues and in acknowledgment of the importance of Mary Maguire's intertextual initiative.

Margaret Gill's sympathetic statement that "the issues that seem to divide us, in fact unite us" is no educational platitude. Fully to acknowledge its import, we have to consider its consequences. As I write, the former country of Yugoslavia is torn by a war as bloody as the horrors perpetrated over thirty years of religious strife in Europe in the seventeenth century. Our news bulletins are crowded with pictures of suffering children, homeless refugees, "ethnic cleansing," and other disasters. Yet each dialogue in this book assumes, as a matter of course, that modern education is carried on in circumstances that make it feasible at least. We all show infinite respect for the young, for the importance of their humane education, as well as a belief that they should be secure and healthy. Yet we know that this is not everywhere possible. Our common understanding is that, as they survive us in the natural run of things, our children will pattern their own solutions to the problems they encounter in the world of their time if we give them scope to learn as well as they can, in freedom from prejudice, intolerance, and fear. But we also know we cannot guarantee these things.

A closer look then reveals that each of us has a concern for a special group, or a minority, in the communities we know well. The details are different in each case, but in our different contexts, we try out the extent of our commitment to what we believe to be the case about language and learning, with the illiterate, the poor, those who are oppressed by their linguistic difference from the standard language. I sense a common awareness of difficulties and pressures in all societies, especially political and financial stringencies in respect to the education of those who have multiple disadvantages. These things shock us out of the assumptions that accompany our privileged comfort. We may speak generally of children "owning their language," but we know what a struggle that can be for those whose social lives are precarious in alienating communities. The example of the Maori scene in Elody Rathgen's piece is important for me. A Zulu lecturer from a training college in South Africa is currently in my tutorial care. At home, she has to work with mothers who cannot read so as to help them to help their children to learn. She is at present in New Zealand to discover how Maori children learn to read English and to discover if the experience is transferable to her homeland. This suggests that, in their "unbounded" form, these talks are already talking to my students. In another place, Henrietta Dombey and I have some responsibility for a new European initiative, in the Institute for the Development of Potentiality in All Children, to which we bring the insights we gain from North American and Australian theory and practice, as well as our home-based experiences.

Then, I think my colleagues and I share a belief that the profession of teaching is about helping children to learn in contexts where understanding and knowledge are seen as social and empirical as well as cognitive and abstract, yet where the relationship of theory and practice is also constantly under review. We stress the importance of children's experience of both the world and of books and other learning resources, their interactions with people, their huge curiosity, and their range of competencies as directly relevant to learning. I doubt if any one of us underestimates the importance of teaching, in the Vygotskian sense of lending our minds out, but we have no time for instruction as a kind of direct transmission ("Learn this, or else . . ."). As our readers, you must have sensed our common notion of knowledge as something brought to life in the minds of learners.

Collaboration is, for us all, an extended and constantly extending concept. In many books and talks, there are condescending references to "collaboration with parents" and to "collaborative learning" where the implication is that others will be glad to go along with what we tell them is necessary or useful. Our shared understanding is different. In education, teachers, parents, educators, and children join in partnerships, as freer, sharing relationships. Henrietta speaks of the "interpenetration of institutions" in the education of teachers; others emphasize the importance of home-school relationships and the respect owed by teachers for the children's lives outside school. Despite our loyalty to our institutions, I doubt if we believe that only schools are successful in helping children to learn. In consequence, we take from each other different ways of engaging parents and children in discussions about learning. In the same way, we act reflexively to rethink how schools can best contribute to the continuing education of the teachers who work in them, not simply in terms of "training," but in the creation of practical theory and theorized practice. As the saying goes, it is better to have thirty years' experience than one year's experience thirty times.

When two teachers talk together, the move to theoretical considerations follows quickly on the shared anecdotes of events. We have all had experience, the privilege, of turning our classroom practice into research inquiry. We also know that research in classrooms has to struggle to "count," where counting usually means the accountancy of statistics and money. The point that classrooms offer "a powerful ethnographic base" is strongly made in several chapters. But we are still experimenting with ethnomethodologies, interactions that extend what can be counted as evidence. This is important for us all. But in the cloud-filled economic weather we all suffer from, very little research is concerned with the children's development over time. Most projects are now funded if they serve a political purpose first and an intellectual one in passing. Our talks included references to research with which we are familiar. But Janet Emig also shows us how teachers may be denied access to enlightenment they need. More practically, teachers who are constrained by program demands now find it more difficult to inquire into alternative theories and practices. In England, where we are struggling to remove the more restrictive impositions of the National Curriculum, classroom research is now channeled into standards and assessment at the very time when our understandings of different modes of inquiry are broadened by influences from other places. And yet, despite all of these drawbacks, the Centre of Language in Primary Education in London has both devised and promoted the most interesting Primary Language Record, a model of collaborative practice with a strong research outreach.

I am particularly touched that my fellow talkers are all women. My fortieth birthday had passed before I realized that, although my schooling had been enriched in many ways, I had been taught mostly by men and expected to learn as if I were a boy. Jane Miller calls this "learned androgyny"; I feel I have some expertise in it. Here we are not teaching feminism; we are confronting issues of power. Janet speaks for all of us when she says, "My work was done over the objections of every senior person in my environment, and that kind of endeavor doesn't have the resonance, the subtlety, that inquiries can have if they are supported." The younger generation of women has not simply entered into a freer inheritance. They have their own problems in this area. They cannot simply align themselves with our experience and think that all will be well. But they may take heart that we have pushed the boundaries back a little.

That women now come together in common enterprises and professional organizations is important, not least because they are in the majority in teaching situations. More important still is that they should be leaders in curriculum and teaching reform. When I was talking about teaching with Mary, I was already aware that the autonomy teachers in England enjoyed was under threat. And so it has proved. We are now learning how to save our "best practice" within the welter of demands made by the National Curriculum. The effort has been of use when it has forced us to rationalize what we think this practice is, and to demonstrate it in ways which make it clear to parents as well as politicians.

It is interesting, surely, that our common concerns arise from our most individualized examples of our work. The worldwide emphasis on writing as composition, instead of scribalism, is a significant point in the history of English teaching, not least because the initiatives began in classrooms before they moved to faculties. We have come to understand the power of talk in learning. Literacy, as a word, rarely appeared in educational writing when I began to teach reading to adults; now it appears most regularly with "crisis." But we are gradually learning that this means a moment of judgment, when we decide what we think is important about it.

For Henrietta and me, these conversations came at a particularly crucial time. As chairperson of the National Association for the Teaching of English, she had the onerous responsibility to review closely what was happening, when the working foundations for the National Curriculum, its position papers, and the proposals for a language model to govern the teaching of English were being promulgated. There were strenuous encounters, some gains, and some considerable losses, as when the innovative practices and materials of the language in the National Curriculum working party were scrapped by governmental orders. But under these imperatives, our understanding was tested *à l'outrance,* and we have not lost heart. For me it was a time when I needed to rethink, fundamentally, my position on literacy, which meant I had to read and write about it. Now I believe that the teaching of reading suffers from the effects of what Richard Rorty calls "final vocabularies," the words we think we cannot do without, but which actually stop us from thinking further, redescribing what we mean and do.

I cannot speak for the others, but I believe the impulse not to stay put began after my exciting experience at the 1989 language arts conference in Montreal. In the middle of the night, just before I was to give my talk, I woke up to the realization that I was, in some ways, shirking the issues I needed to confront. As Henrietta so cogently says, I was being anxious to please instead of expressing what I thought to be the case. So I rewrote the talk then and there, less neatly, because I knew that the best thing one does in education is to be honest with one's colleagues, to take them into one's thinking, and to expect honest responses. I don't know how it was for the listeners, but I began some important new dialogue with myself. The experience has been repeated in writing this, in the hope that something of the same has come to you from these conversations.

Learning must always be some kind of dialogue, otherwise the life of the mind is a series of vain repetitions. My gratitude for this book goes to its editor, my colleague contributors, and to its dialogic readers. Now talk on.

Selected Bibliography
for Margaret Meek Spencer

The books listed below were published under the name Margaret Meek.

The Cool Web: The Pattern of Children's Reading (co-edited with A. Warlow and G. Barton). 1977. London: The Bodley Head.

Learning to Read. 1982. London: The Bodley Head.

Achieving Literacy: Longitudinal Studies of Adolescents Learning to Read. 1983. London: Routledge and Kegan Paul.

Opening Moves:Work in Progress in the Study of Children's Language Development (editor). 1983. Bedford Way Papers 17. London: Institute of Education, University of London.

How Texts Teach What Readers Learn. 1988. Stroud, U.K.: Thimble Press.

On Being Literate. 1992. Portsmouth, N.H.: Heinemann.

Janet Emig

M y interview with Janet Emig took place on a Saturday morning in the family room of a friend's home, the day after she spoke in April 1986 at Springboards, the Quebec annual English Language Arts conference. I wrote to Janet a month before her scheduled visit to Montreal and requested an interview with her. I appreciated the warmth and candidness of her response in a telephone conversation a few days before the conference:"I'm game if you're game," she stated. In our Montreal conversation, she talks about inquiry as conversation and her view of conversations as alternative forms of organizing ourselves. I deliberately began with reference to her keynote address at the 1978 Writing Conference at Carleton University and her seminal paper, "Inquiry Paradigms," which is included in the edited collection of her essays in the book The Web of Meaning.

Scanning the U.S. Scene

The Tacit Dimension: The Inevitability of a Multidisciplinary Approach to Writing Research

MARY: Janet, I remember how excited I was the first time I heard you speak at the 1978 Ottawa conference. You talked about the tacit tradition and the inevitability of a multidisciplinary approach to writing research. Let's just start there. What does this paper mean to you now ten years later?

JANET: I thought probably it was an important act, to try to make some acknowledgment of what I elected to call our ancestors. I am always made nervous by delineating any corpus. I think there are hazards in composition, as there prove to be in literature, of identifying something that we might call the canon or those who belong to the canon. At the same time, I found so many commonalties among a group of scholars that I thought it was valuable for us to highlight them as a way of beginning to appreciate that we indeed were beginning to develop into what, for better or worse, we call a discipline.

Knowing the Modes of Inquiry: The Second Generation of Scholars

MARY: Where do you see writing as a discipline now, and where are we going?

JANET: In the United States, the current excitement for me comes from what I'm calling rather arbitrarily the second generation of scholars in writing research. I think they bring to their work a depth and a breadth and a consideration of inquiries. This is something that those of us who were there at the beginning either did not have or did not bring to play upon our writing and research. I mean particularly the immense values of training and insight into a number of literary theories that simply weren't even present when some of us began to write about writing. Literature, at the time we were writing about writing in the States, was a concern of New Criticism. We were carefully not told about Louise Rosenblatt. She had difficulty finding a forum during a period of one of the disgraceful moments in the history of English studies. Now one can trust that a writing researcher will be acquainted not only with New Criticism, but with Marxism, Feminism, Structuralism, Poststructuralism, and all the possibilities that are contained therein, for interplay between those theories and the theories that we are developing in rhetoric.

Therefore, I think the sophistication of training is far, far greater. More recently, however, I've been disturbed by the overcommitment by many of the young scholars to a single theoretical point of view, with the outcome which I regard as the balkanization of English studies: contentious camps, with no conversations beyond the tent flaps, only the lobbing of shells. Another problem with many doctrinaire positions is that they play hell with prose style. As an instance, see the polysyllabic glop of too many Marxists, unreadable and surely no model for their students.

I'd add that there is now a more generous definition of what inquiry is or can be. The younger researchers know this and are comfortable in doing a historical study or a speculative study along with doing an experimental study. They know more and, by knowing the modes of inquiry, they can do something more sophisticated like a combined study. These studies tend to have portions that are historical, along with portions that are speculative, along with portions that may be experimental.

Someone whose work interests me particularly at the moment is Louise Phelps at Syracuse. What I'm struck by in the work of Louise is that her grounding in philosophy is very deep. Consequently, she has the ability to see the possible connection and relevance of someone like Paul Ricoeur for the teaching of composition. Along with this is a trust, a feeling of responsibility, that to espouse theory means simultaneously to try to enact it. Therefore, the writing center that she's devised at Syracuse is an effort at the exemplification of a theory which she believes in. It is a democratic enterprise in that all members who participate in the center help in formulating the curriculum theory that they will do. So to proceed in writing is to regard composition as an ongoing conversation. I think it's accurate to say that she regards her approach as being somehow connected with being a woman. The way she elects to conduct inquiry is not confrontational, but rather is a shared speculation. This is what makes a big difference. She and I are meeting in two weeks to write the prospectus of a new anthology, called *The Feminine*

Principles of Opposition, in which we like to speculate: Do women teach composition differently in some way? Do we do research differently? I think the answer to both is yes.

MARY: I think some do and wonder why others don't. What do you speculate would be the difference?

JANET: I think we're initially more willing to trust the expressive mode. Consequently, emanating from that is a willingness to trust the role of narrative in thinking. We trust story and storying as a way of knowing more readily, I think.

MARY: Within the traditional research paradigm, there is still resistance to this mode of inquiry. Let's come back to the comment you made a bit earlier; you mentioned that Louise Rosenblatt had a difficult time trying to find a forum for her writing. As it speaks to me, her writing is very much in the expressive mode.

JANET: It is indeed! And again it seems to me to be the female principle. First one must allow and trust the response of any other to any experience. This may come about from parenting, whether or not it is literal parenting or parenting as in teaching. Whatever form it takes, there must be legitimacy given to whatever we first make of our own experiences. We can't attribute that to feminism alone. One can think of Dewey. He was the one who said to us to trust and believe in our own experiences, and how the shapes follow the experiences into transforming largely how we reflect on what happened. So emphasis is on trust, trusting reflection on any form, on espousing what I'm calling, perhaps too tightly, the feminist principle.

MARY: Let's come back to the contribution that the second-generation researchers are making. Besides Louise Phelps, who would be some other people who are working within this mode?

JANET: I think another person would be David Bartholomae and there is Anthony Petrosky at the University of Pittsburgh. Another feature of their work is what they write. For example, Petrosky is a practicing and award-winning poet. So his knowledge of writing is what I call primary knowledge. Both he and David also have the kind of training I've been talking about. They don't see artificial lines drawn between considering a rhetorical problem and considering a literary problem. There is in a sense a continuum between texts and theories. We've been very arbitrary in our prior divisions.

Storying as a Way of Knowing: Shapes That Follow Experiences

MARY: Speaking of texts and the expressive mode, I'm playing with a concept which for now I'm calling the commanded text and the preferred text, in the sense that there are always two texts competing for the same space on the written page. There's the commanded text—a text a person feels obliged to write to please someone such as a teacher or an editor, or to get on, or what have you. There's the preferred text, which really is the self coming through in whatever mode is chosen. I'm wondering if you see these second-generation researchers changing "the texts" of our scholarly journals, which I see largely as a canon of commanded texts. I'm thinking of *Research in the Teaching of English,* which my graduate students say they read only if they have to. Will the texts of our journals tend to take on a new dimension?

JANET: I very much hope so. I've spoken about this elsewhere. At the four C's convention in Atlanta, three women scholars from Towson State in Maryland were discussing a new curriculum they were devising. One woman, as a part of what she was doing in writing in science, took a look at what our Nobel Prize laureates in the States truly did in their current writing. I don't remember exactly how many she interviewed—sixty I think. What she was struck by was their total comfort with using first person, their total comfort with using extended metaphor, and their total comfort with using narrative. If that's the case, then we should eventually become comfortable in our own journals with having accounts, stories, poems, poems as theory, narratives as theory, extended metaphors as theory. I very much hope that will happen.

MARY: That to me has a lot of implications for the so-called essayist tradition that's so deeply embedded not just in our journals, but in our educational system and research tradition. This makes me think back to someone you mentioned earlier, Paul Ricoeur, and how in his book *Time and Narrative* he argues that if you are working within a narrative mode, the task becomes one of choosing from what temporal stance you're going to view whatever it is you're looking at. So I'm wondering if you, as a first-generation researcher looking at the work of second-generation researchers, would comment on what kinds of stances you see us taking. Through your work on the composing process, you broke out of a paradigm in the early 70s when people were not working within this kind of a liberatory mode of inquiry. So what stance will you yourself take now?

JANET: Well, as I think I said at the end of *The Web of Meaning,* I was going off to write poetry. I am currently writing far more poetry than I am writing theory. I think it's possible to cross those modes, to write theory as poetry and poetry as theory. Our poet James Merrill, in his "Scripts for the Pageant" and some other recent work, has portions of his poetry which are the most profound little essays on how language began, how language is used. Then we get over our fixities about what mode is which. T. S. Eliot's *Four Quartets* is a very great work on the creative process. We should start encouraging ourselves and others to cross modes. Now whether or not I'm going to do that I don't quite know. What I'm currently writing is a poem; it looks as if it's going to be an extremely long, sad poem to do with a number of endangered species in the world, plants and animals. It is called "Goodbye." So that's what I'm doing now. I hope others who are writing about writing as poets or short storyists will continue to do so.

Knowing Writing: Trusting Reflection on Form

MARY: I'm even more curious about what actually made you risk-take in the 70s and break out into a new mode of inquiry, especially for a dissertation and which obviously has had tremendous influence on how we now look at writing.

JANET: Well, I think I've said this before, but I had to express my total shock, surprise, and delight that anything came of that venture. Because at that time I had no notion it would receive any acceptance whatsoever. I broke out because of the mismatch between how I wrote and how I was reading in handbooks about how I should write. I just was very lucky that I did not have too many teachers who believed the handbooks. I was very fortunate in college. My teachers of writing were themselves distinguished writers. My senior honors adviser was a remarkable British novelist, Joyce Horner, perhaps best known for a novel called *Greyhound on a Leash.* So when we talked writing, we talked as senior colleague to junior colleague. Consequently, I didn't meet these terrible handbooks until later when I began to teach. I suppose I watched the wrenching my students were experiencing trying to cope with the handbooks. At the same time, I was teaching in a very enlightened high school where the superintendent had read about class size. As an experiment, he had two of us who taught tenth and eleventh grade be reduced to only a hundred students a day and gave us the other two periods in the day for conferencing. This was in the early 50s; it was a remarkable thing. I quickly put aside the handbooks because in the writing and the conferencing we had vivid accounts of process. So it was watching my students, watching myself, and being terribly lucky in the education I had.

I also somehow intuitively knew that Chomsky, who was absolutely the leading intellectual figure when I was at Harvard, was not entirely, but partially, wrong. I was on the editorial board of the *Harvard Education Review.* Three of us, Helen Popp, James Fleming, and I wanted to do a special issue. I cannot tell you the battles we had to include the work of Becker and Young with tagmemics, which somehow implied an interest in discourse that was not sentence bound, that was not Chomsky. I think we've been confirmed as time has passed. I don't mean this self-pityingly, but I have grown concerned with some recent accounts of my work. The young authors seem to think that I was writing in a propitious context. I was not. My work was done over the objections of every senior person in my environment, and that kind of endeavor does not have the resonance, the subtlety, that inquiries can have if they're supported. It was inadequate; but I think it could not help but be, given the environment that I was in.

MARY: As you have talked about your experience of being a secondary school English teacher and breaking into the world of research, I see you saying that there have been deeply embedded boundaries in terms of what is permissible to enter into our knowing and inquiries. As we approach the 90s, do you think we're making fast headway in terms of breaking these boundaries?

JANET: No, I think we're making slow headway, but I think we are making headway. It's so difficult to know the effects, say in the States, of the National Writing Project. But when I characterize it to myself, I think it's the single most important curricular reform movement that I know of in American education. Its visible effects are impressive, but I think its invisible effects are deeper and longer term. When I think about the writing projects across North America, I get very heartened. But when I look at the opposite, that is, what portion of teachers in our countries elect to be members of our professional organizations and who elect to hear and listen, then I grow depressed. If we take the total teacher population in the States and our membership in the National Council of Teachers of English, I think we only reach 20 percent of the teachers. Is that representative of the situation in Canada?

MARY: I don't really know. I think it probably would look different in different provinces because education is such a provincial affair, and it's confounded even further by the bilingual nature of our schools. Secondary and university teachers connect more to the Canadian Council of Teachers of English as a national organization, while the elementary teachers have traditionally affiliated with local councils of the International Reading Association. I think in Nova Scotia there has been tremendous headway in the whole-language movement and writing as process movement, also in British Columbia and Alberta.

The pessimistic boundary that we're experiencing in Canada is that many ministries of education have decided to separate the curriculum developers from the evaluators. From my own perspective, just as an aside here, that's a big mistake. If we don't win that battle on evaluation and standardized testing, we can have as many movements and theories as possible, but the crunch comes when we are putting a label or a number or a comment on a report card.

JANET: Yes, I would agree. In the States I'm most heartened by what's happening in California, where the teachers themselves are the source of the assessment for the state of California. Consequently, the assessment is in the hands of teachers, and when the assessment is in the hands of teachers, so then the curriculum in the most vivid important sense is in the hands of teachers. Teachers can begin to make connections between the assessment that they themselves have done based on their own experience in the classroom, and the best of what they know, and the research.

Holding Conversations:
Alternative Forms of
Organizing Ourselves

MARY: What do you see as possible directions for more collaborative kinds of relationships between university people who are sometimes perceived as the theorists and the researchers, and classroom teachers who tend to see themselves as being the practitioners? My own view is that teachers are also theorists.

JANET: My view as well is that teachers are theorists and at times test theorists. Shirley Brice Heath at our coalition meeting last summer suggested that to have an effect she thinks we need to organize our institutes, our training ventures, differently. Our institutes should be wider representations of the community. Our present institutes should include the university researcher, the classroom teacher, the parent, the administrator; all these groups, and probably the students as well, should be represented and talk together. If we're going to be effective we need to find different ways of meeting and holding conversations.

MARY: What mechanisms do you see for having these conversations emerge? How can we do this?

JANET: Within the States, I think the greatest likelihood of conversations coming about is from the grass roots, from affiliates in the cities, in regions, and so on. I don't see them as top down; I see them bottom up. I think they simply should be encouraged and supported by all the professional organizations in any way possible. The difficulty is finding funding, particularly in arrangements such as ours at the moment. With our current administration, it is exclusively a top-down kind of reward system that has been promoted.

MARY: These top-down administrations are really the people who are making the judgments and the decisions about evaluation. If evaluation is going to be in the hands of teachers, what does this mean other than teachers just sharing their results or their evidence at conferences or institutes? I mean, would you see something else having to emerge? I guess what I'm getting at is really an issue of power.

JANET: It is an issue of power. I see teachers organizing themselves so that as professionals they are in charge of curriculum and teaching. We need more inquiry into different kinds of organizations from what we now have. I don't know exactly the form that they would wish to take, but the teachers will be the initiators; the teachers will be the espousers. I wish I could envision something more clearly. I hope someone does. I think it's crucial that we apply our imagination to the alternative forms of organizing ourselves. It won't be a union and it won't be a national teacher organization; it will be organized conceptually.

MARY: I had reason to hope this is starting to happen when I was out in Vancouver last week. LOMCIRA, the Lower Mainland Council of the International Reading Association, IRA, organized a mini-conference for elementary school teachers on whole language. On a Saturday morning well over three hundred turned out and they had to turn two hundred people away. Now, I've seen that happen in pockets in the States as well. Seeing what marvelous work was being done in Vancouver made me think of how Montreal teachers could know about this, and Vancouver teachers know about Montreal teachers. How can we begin to envision more networks for disseminating teachers' work and celebrating what teachers are doing?

JANET: I think we're going to have to use other means than physical transportation of bodies. One is telecommunications. I'm excited by the "Breadnet" effort from the Breadloaf School, whereby the teacher researchers, whom Dixie Goswami is encouraging, are consulting with one another by this means. So they're staying in touch; there are conference calls. I don't think we've begun to use the technology that's currently available to us, the technology that corporations use daily and matter-of-factly, to connect ourselves in the way we need to get connected.

MARY: Where would you see computers in all of this?

JANET: Ah, that's another possibility. Jeff Golub from the University of Washington was at our coalition meeting. I think we shocked him by our naïveté, and by our not knowing that there are all kinds of ways of keeping us connected that are inexpensive and that teachers could make immediate use of. We need to trust the media specialist in our midst to help us with this problem.

MARY: What would your response be to the computer software programs? I mean those things that are really not based on what we now know about language and learning, or writing and reading, or even thinking, but are really no more than electronic workbooks.

JANET: I'm very concerned about that. But this reminds me of a time about twenty years ago with programmed learning. Then, programmed learning was to be the panacea and now it's the software, but most of the software materials are benighted. They're dealing with a view of learning and teaching that's been discredited. There's a terrible time lag, and so the software can just be another variant of workbooks.

MARY: You were talking earlier about how our life histories tend to influence how we view, and how we work, and what we bring to the teaching act. Looking back, and since we're on the subject of computers now, do you think that your study of the composing process would have taken another dimension had computers been in fashion then?

JANET: One of the most marked advantages of computers and word processors is that they make so clear to us what is composition and what is something else; they show the actual symbolic manipulation and transformation of language. Anything the computer does, can do, without our direct participation probably isn't central to the composing act. In other words, I think the value is to give us a clear definition of writing. As I once said rather awkwardly, the motoric act is such an intrusion for many children that to take that out, to eliminate it, is to help them immensely. If indeed we learn from writing, if writing is learning, if there is the interacting cycle of eye, hand, and brain, if the presence of a text that can be immediately transformed is visible to the eye, I think it is an immense asset for many, many children learning to write and for many adults as well.

MARY: That's interesting. How about those writers who still prefer to write with paper and pen? I often encounter this from my own teachers who still like the pen and paper. There are times when I may sit down and write directly onto the computer and then other times when I want that connection with my yellow pad and HB pencil. What makes the writing, the composition, different? Or is it really different? Why do we do that?

JANET: I'm just beginning to grow comfortable with using the computer, so you're talking with a novice. I must have a sculpting visceral relation with words when I'm writing poetry. Even now, though, I'm beginning to revise poems on the processor. I can never imagine a time when I will wholly write poems on the computer, because as I said poetry is sculpted; it has to be if it's tactile.

MARY: Are there then modes of discourse you'd say that lend themselves more readily to being composed at the computer?

JANET: I guess I'm implying that, but I don't know whether it's the case. It would certainly be interesting to speculate about.

Making Connections: Making Interdisciplinary Interconnections

MARY: Yes, and what interests me is how young children learn to write on the computer. I began teaching as a secondary school English teacher and now find myself interested in preschoolers and how literary criticism has something to say to language development and early reading and early writing. I wonder if we could come back to the topic of literary criticism. Who are the key literary critics that have made an influence on your thinking about the composing process?

JANET: Well, I've already mentioned Louise Rosenblatt. First of all she's a personal friend whom I see often, to my great pleasure. She herself is making these interconnections more and more. She has a new chapter coming out in a handbook on English language arts research, and she also has a paper that she just recently did for the Center on Writing in California, showing the interconnections that she sees. Louise makes me cautious because, as you know, she's already written one article about a terminological rescue operation on her notion of transaction. I'm loath to make the analogies too broad between what she's doing and what we're doing.

MARY: Okay. Would you extend the ideas we have been talking about, such as the value of literary criticism to the reading-writing relationship?

JANET: Absolutely. Yes indeed. For the second-generation scholars, with their dual training in rhetorical research and literary research, the possibilities of exciting, sensible connections being made are far, far greater.

MARY: What you're saying is that the new research that will be emerging will need to be interdisciplinary if it's going to be coherent.

JANET: Yes, I see no alternative to that. And of course we haven't even begun to talk about the interconnections with what we're learning about how the brain works, the biological basis of learning. I think another formidable task for the researchers is to keep up with what's going on in neurology.

MARY: If we can just engage in some speculative thinking here right now: Would you predict that in the next generation of research we'll find that how we think is a unitary process, although we can have different strategies that we may deploy in different ways for whatever purposes? Or do you think that we'll find out that it's not a unitary process?

JANET: I find that very difficult to say. I just don't think I know enough to speak about that.

Connecting Ourselves: Reconnecting with Our Stories

MARY: In the Montreal inner-city schools, many teachers that I work with have many different ethnic groups in their classrooms. I guess the reason why that question interests me is that, when we see these cultural differences, a question comes to mind: Do we see children as more alike or more different? I think the answer to that question has a lot of implications for the ways in which we will look at teaching and learning.

JANET: In New Jersey we supposedly have over ninety language groups. For education then it's valuable to hold a hypothesis of commonalties.

MARY: I think so. But then how do we deal with differences in classroom settings? You mentioned that narrative is one of the primary modes of learning and knowing. It seems to me that we've really lost that art of storying in our classrooms. How can we bring it alive?

JANET: I think we allow these magnificent multiple stories that our children bring to our classrooms, allow them legitimacy inside the classroom by genuinely showing that we want to hear these stories. I'd think we would need to learn much more about what Robert Kaplan at the University of Southern California calls contrastive rhetoric. We really need to make far more cross-cultural studies about definitions of rhetoric in various groups, because the definitions are different and the ideas are different. There seems to be quite clearly a different way of organization for a piece of Chinese discourse, from a piece of Arabic discourse, and from a piece of North American discourse. We are assuming an essayist tradition that is not shared by many of the students who are coming to us. Their presence will enlarge our definition of modes and ways of knowing in the classroom, if we are going to honor the ways of knowing they bring to us, which are disparate and exciting and, frequently, I think, narrative.

MARY: Let's relate this further to the school context, be that a university setting, secondary school, or elementary school. How can we have these discourse modes emerge from classrooms, given our current structure? Does this mean that the whole structure of schooling needs to be transformed?

JANET: Seems that way, does it not? It seems as if our skilled teachers who have the most primary connection with the students will have to be the ones to help tell us to ask the questions that we need to be asking, and show the ways in which the rest of us can help them to work in classrooms with greater imagination and thought.

MARY: You've been doing some cross-age, cross-cultural work with older writers.

JANET: I'm just beginning a project. In 1983 I taught a handful of older Americans in Florida, and next month I'm going to start a small research project in Florida. I am very interested in entering retirement homes, which are desperate places in many parts of North America, at least so it seems to me. My hypothesis is very simple—that reconnecting with our own stories, whatever age we are, is a source of physical as well as mental improved health. I am going to start with a case study of a single woman, I think. And then move out to a writing group, and then try to establish writing groups in retirement homes. I'll develop a model that I hope others will be interested in using.

MARY: I'd like to relate that to your earlier metaphor, the first-generation and the second-generation researchers. What possibilities do you see for that model breaking into the school system with young authors, our third genera-tion of researchers, working into retirement homes and bringing retirement people into the schools?

JANET: There are all kinds of possibilities; there are all kinds of exciting cross-generational activities going on all over North America. Wonderfully imaginative teachers are arranging grandparenting connections with others in retirement homes. These are very exciting ventures. It is not only giving the children the grandparents they don't have, but it is connecting them with history that they've lost by our truncated or our dispersed families.

MARY: What do you see as the likely outcome in the next decades of more and more research studies that are cross-generational?

JANET: I think first of all we'd be establishing a new and happy definition of what a family is, and that is a group of people who are cheerfully and generatively literate together. It's a definition we've had in our past; it could be a definition we'll have in our future. The membership might just be a little different; it would not be necessarily blood connections. The second outcome I think is political and very important. We're having trouble in the States with a great many bond issues failing in communities where children have grown and gone away. This kind of interconnection could well change this, if it were broad enough. The interaction between the child and the older adult would immediately lead the older adult to want the best for the child, which would mean support of education in whatever form it would take. I think that if it works, perhaps fewer bond issues would fail.

MARY: Perhaps this would address one of Shirley Brice Heath's concerns and offer hope for the survival of American schools. Would you say that?

JANET: I would say that, if it were a wide enough spread. We have such trouble organizing ourselves, but I do think therein lies a possibility.

MARY: What advice would you give to what we might call the third generation of researchers?

JANET: I guess my general advice would be to both trust and risk: trust what's emerging about what we're learning, about the legitimacy of many ways of knowing, and risk venturing forth in alternate ways of setting forth what we're learning. I mean there are currently some curious anomalies, for example, to have an account of storying presented as an expository essay. As I said in Ottawa two years ago, if we were doing a cell, one of the empty categories would be a form of inquiry which we might call a narrative on narrative. I think that would be an exciting way to go. I know that generation two and generation one in some instances will have to be persuaded of the legitimacy of this. But I think research is always an act of rhetoric and is always an act of persuasion, particularly if we're going to have new ventures and new inquiries. We simply set ourselves that task and know that persuasion in that sense is part of what we do.

MARY: How do you convince graduate students to do that when for some their concern is to be safe and not risk?

JANET: Well, one way is to make it safe inside, and a second is to reward divergent actions and behavior. I mean offer the serious reward, which is that dissertations will be accepted. We will say that this form of inquiry will be accepted as a closing, intellectual, conceptual exercise in the university.

MARY: Do you see this then as closing the gap between what seemed to be dichotomies and camps in the research field? In a sense there are the hard-core empirical researchers versus the naturalistic and ethnographic research-ers, sometimes mislabeled mush-headed researchers by some empiricists.

JANET: Yes. I don't know of anything more demanding than to acquire thick documentation about a single act, process, or person. What's soft-headed about that eludes me, but I hope that these artificial and perhaps destructive dichotomies can be bridged. And they will be bridged by students only if those of us who have the privilege of being in positions of power can be as imaginative as our students are. I don't mean this in any condescending way; I mean this in a parental way, a protective way.

MARY: Do you think then this will mean that we need new tools for look-ing and how we look?

JANET: I think indeed we do. We will have to invent them as we need them, or the other possibility is they are there and we must look to other disciplines to tell us how they inquire, just as we did with ethnography and found help there for ourselves.

MARY: So in a sense it's playing with forms of discourse.

JANET: Playing with forms of discourse which I again would characterize as rhetorical, active process.

MARY: How can we convince secondary and elementary school teachers of this? I can see that persuasion would work in the university setting.

JANET: Teachers themselves I think could be persuaded by experienc-ing the power of their own use of language. Any of the institutes that I was talking about earlier, for example the National Writing Institute, do this. When teachers find their own voices in their own speaking and writing, they are persuaded of the value of the narrative mode. It must be this way; it must be primary.

MARY: So children and their teachers derive the written language system from what they experience of it.

JANET: From what they experience indeed of it, and that experiencing must be sponsored by all those of us who have the opportunity to sponsor it.

MARY: What do you do with someone who refuses to write? Who doesn't want to experience it, who won't risk experiencing it?

JANET: Even though I think there are unique values to writing, I think we must at least initially acknowledge and allow, as Howard Gardner and Vera John-Steiner and others are pointing out to us, that there are alternate forms of mind, that there are alternate intelligences and ways of knowing, and be far more generous than we've been thus far in allowing students to begin in the symbolic modes in which they feel the greatest comfort, to which they feel the greatest allegiance. Then, if possible, we should move them out because of what we believe are some unique values to writing in different modes and be far more generous in what we allow as response.

MARY: I'm thinking of a comment from Clifford Geertz that we must allow people to traffic in the symbolic modes available in the community.

JANET: Exactly, otherwise they are not going to learn how to orchestrate these for their own purposes when they need to know them as learners throughout their lives.

MARY: Yes, is there anything else that you'd like to say in closing.

JANET: Just my pleasure in being here and my excitement about what I'm learning about the whole-language movement here in Quebec, and hoping that what's going on here can be widely shared, so that in the States we learn more and more about the kind of imaginative curriculum to which you've all committed yourselves.

Different Emphases in the International Conversation

Mary, what I so like about the cluster of women you have interviewed is the orchestration. In my opinion, we have contributed to different emphases in the international conversation.

For me, Margaret Gill's contributions are political and enactive. With Bob Shafer and a few others, she has served as a major organizer and propeller of IFTE, the International Federation for the Teaching of English. Like you, she has acted on the importance of orchestration by urging us to hold our conferences at many venues and by always arranging for conversations at almost every meeting.

She also knows what works and what doesn't in the classroom. Like Aviva Freedman, Margaret appreciates and she enacts. Note how seamlessly she alludes to a range of research. She is a very major source of our professional energy.

As I read Margaret Meek Spencer's marvelous interview, once again I was struck by how differently most of my British colleagues proceed from most of my U.S. colleagues on major matters of literacy. The key comment here is, "What always worries me is that people who don't write teach writing, and people who don't read teach reading. It does seem a bit loony if you were to invite a non-piano player teacher to teach your child to play the piano."

I think I envy her, and Nancy Martin, Jimmy Britton, Harold Rosen, and the others, for seemingly not having to fight against what is still a powerful view in the U.S. of how to teach reading. You know, regarding learning to read as some kind of CIA affair—clandestine, alien, overelaborate, paranoid— a matter of breaking THE CODE. In the U.K. the approach to reading seems so much more nonmechanistic, relaxed. I attribute the difference to the more organic roles of writing and reading in their teachers' lives.

I am stunned by how many of the supposed authorities on reading in the U.S. don't read, other than their dreary journals; or regard true reading, which is of course reading for delight and self-deepening, as an appurtenance they actually tag, dismissively, "recreational reading." If I were to ask too many I know how they like Tan, Helprin, Hempel, Smiley, Rush, Salter, Graham, Cliff, Silko, Erdrich, Leavitt, they wouldn't know anyone I was talking about, although we seem to have here a little cluster of our recent Pulitzer Prize and National Book Award winners.

When I describe our work on writing processes or reader-response to genuinely literate friends at parties, I watch them trying to frame, nonrudely, the question: Aren't we dealing with commonplaces? And the answer is, yes. Writing is a process, yes. We respond personally to what we read, yes. That, in North America, we have had to raise to the status of theories what every literate person already knows is an indictment of our parochial, atomistic, condescending, Puritanic approaches. How did the Brits manage to keep Cromwell out of it?

I admire as well Margaret Spencer's open discussion of class and its effects upon the learning and teaching of literacy. The United States is a classed society too, although we are even more hypocritical than the British about the chasms and the insuperable difficulties for most in leaping across. Note how we are dismantling our public school system now that many of our fine citizens have determined only the poor attend, especially in our cities.

What's striking to me is how vividly analogous the British situation regarding national curriculums and assessment that Henrietta Dombey described (in what, 1988?) is to our scene in the States today. The political talk, at least among the Republicans, is all of standardization and national norms and goals. There are major efforts to devise single tests to measure competency in literacy of all sorts, verbal, mathematical, scientific.

And the irony, as usual, is that the most sophisticated research and theory are taking us in the opposite direction from this majority agenda. At the very time colleges and universities are stressing the mosaic of human experience— I like the Canadian metaphor more than our polysyllabic *multiculturalism*— many politicians and members of our white majority want to return to some fantasized Golden Age of monolithic values and a single, unquestioned civic identity. At the very time that majority wants a single test, Henry Higgins-like, by which to judge all children no matter their family of origin—you know, why can't the Hispanics be more like us?—our citizens of color are becoming the majority populations. And the most serious students of assessment are promulgating multiple modes of evaluation, such as the three *p*'s: performance (solo), portfolios (solo), and projects (both solo and collaborative).

My questions now, and I currently don't have any British informants, are: How is the National Curriculum faring now, and how would Henrietta assess its success or failure?

Aviva fulfills my deepest definitions for being a feminist. She appreciates (most men don't realize how active a verb that is) with extraordinary prescience and creativity. She stays grounded in actualities: she is never lost in untethered abstractions. And she builds communities, locally, nationally, and internationally.

As I wrote in *Web,* I still remember the first Carleton conference Aviva and Ian Pringle orchestrated as the most electric in which I ever participated. It would be difficult to overstate the importance of the two Carleton conferences for forwarding the international conversation. We had to talk with one another; we had to listen—well, most of us felt we did.

I think I may regard the opportunity she provided me at the second conference as even more important than the first. The theme, as many will recall, was "The Issues That Divide Us." Now to appropriately deal with that theme requires a certain rhetorical stance, the agonistic. And although many regard the agonistic as a male subgenre, as often the only female academic in my environment I had to learn it early to survive. My opposite number in a series of what I—and I think, she—regarded as a series of debates to highlight differences was Carl Bereiter, who had written that essay about levels of inquiry. Now, as we used to say in my old neighborhood, I owed him one for his very nasty public behavior to me at the first conference. Actually, I owed him two if we count my feelings about Distar, which I regard as a racist disgrace. This isn't to say that I haven't admired his later work, particularly that long piece on composition as conversation that he co-authored with Marlene Scardamalia, a woman.

And so I took him on. I don't think that he had prepared for our encounter, an insult not so much to me as to some colleagues who had traveled halfway round the world to attend. At the end of the encounter he looked like a disheveled rooster. Over the years young women who were in the audience have come up to me at other conventions to thank me. They claimed they had never before seen a woman academic truly take on a male counterpart in a public arena, and just how yeasty they found the experience. Aviva arranged that exchange very knowingly.

I agree with her comment about some of the CCC conferences in recent years, both concerning the careerism and the theoretical extremism. Actually, these are intertwined, I think. Many young U.S. academics fear rightly that they could be punished in their own departments and colleges for public intellectual boldness, particularly if they espouse a position that diverges from some current intellectual norm or supposed accepted position. Given the fractionalization in most North American departments of English, it must be exhausting trying to fathom how to survive, by which I mean, of course, how to become tenured.

Elody Rathgen's interview sponsors in me comments on three issues: who belongs to our professional organizations and why; related gender issues; and, finally, ESL and the work going on in its name.

NCTE, like NZATE, represents only about 20 percent of English teachers in the United States (I don't know what percentage of Canadian teachers belongs either to NCTE or to CATE). Why so few, proportionately? I think for two reasons: one, both groups represent what were once called liberal values in our schools and societies while the schools and societies themselves grow more and more reactionary, to me frighteningly so. The 90s feel like the 30s, with the threat of fascism again hovering over the earth. Clannishness, ethnic enclaves, censorship, extreme self-interest, hatred of the different, literal violence, all these seem to dominate current historical changes. Our professional groups, worldwide, call for conversation among cultures, the honoring of divergence, words not blows, the presence of democracy—minority stances, alas.

Also, the powerful role of women in these organizations makes these groups politically unacceptable to those committed to patriarchies. Now for a very unpopular comment: we find even among ourselves subtle but powerful forms of sexism. Take the matter of attribution. Here is Emig's law: $A = M(W + 1)$ or the first man after the woman who initiates a concept or a theory gets the credit: Iser rather than Rosenblatt for reader-response.

The Wellesley Center on Women has recently published a study about how schools steadily favor boys in North America. Clearly, the situation obtains as well in Australia and New Zealand. Countries recently decolonized have, I think, an even more difficult time than the U.S. in sponsoring equity between the sexes, because England was so very heavy-handedly the Victorian father, so unrelievedly patriarchal. Note how almost inescapable that pre-World War I curriculum has proved throughout the Commonwealth.

Regarding linguistic diversity, I think that Geneva Smitherman has made the most exciting recommendation. She suggests that it is not enough for children to be bilingual. Rather, all children should be at least trilingual: knowing and using not only the language of nurture and the majority language of communication within a culture, but also one that simply extends their sense of the world and its almost infinite diversity.

Selected Bibliography
for Janet Emig

The Composing Process of Twelfth Graders. 1971. NCTE Research Report No. 13. Urbana, Ill.: National Council of Teachers of English.

The Tacit Tradition: The Inevitability of a Multidisciplinary Approach to Writing Research. 1980. In *Reinventing the Rhetorical Tradition,* edited by A. Freedman and I. Pringle, 9–17. Conway, Ark.: L & S Books.

Writing as a Mode of Learning; and Non-Magical Thinking: Presenting Writing Developmentally in Schools. In *The Web of Meaning: Essays on Writing, Teaching, Learning, and Thinking,* edited by D. Goswami and M. Butler, 122–144. Upper Montclair, N.J.: Boynton/Cook.

Aviva Freedman

*O*ver the years I have enjoyed many formal and informal conversations with Aviva Freedman because of the short distance between Montreal and Ottawa. All my conversations with her have been illuminating and intellectually challenging. Our conversation in this book took place on a sunny summer afternoon in her office after the TESOL summer institute in August 1990 at Carleton University. Once again I was stimulated by the clarity of her thinking and her artful ability to articulate her thoughts about complex issues. She reflects back on the significance of the 1978 and 1986 international conferences at Carleton that she co-chaired with Ian Pringle. She looks ahead to some major issues we might address as a profession in the 90s. Intriguing and challenging are Aviva's views about engaging in oppositional discourse, which by her definition is critically reading the issues, our words, responses, worlds, public and private realities.

Reinventing the Discipline—Reinventing Ourselves

Reflecting on Issues and Making Choices

MARY: Two very significant events in which you were involved in organizing at Carleton influenced my own theoretical perspective, one being the very exciting 1978 conference on writing and the second being the IFTE 1986 conference on "The Issues That Divide Us." Let's take a retrospective look back to 1978.

AVIVA: Sure, that 1978 conference that Ian Pringle and I organized for CCTE was a significant moment for me as well. Preparing for the conference and then experiencing it as it unfolded corroborated for me the reality of a new, or should I say renewed, discipline: writing research or rhetoric or composition theory. (I'm still not happy with any of these designations.) I remember teaching composition, or at least trying to teach freshman composition in the U.S. in the mid to late 60s, and trying to get some kind of handle on this amorphous and neglected entity, trotting regularly into class with my McCrimmon under my arm and feeling so inadequate and so deceitful.

Then my life underwent one of those discontinuities that women typically face, and I found myself, seven years later (or light-years later, depending on whose calendar you're looking at), in a different time and a different place, looking at composition again, or at least at the teaching of composition. Two children and four moves later, I had turned up at Carleton's doorstep and had found myself a job coordinating a research project undertaken at Carleton for the provincial Ministry of Colleges and Universities and looking at the teaching of writing. My task included reviewing all the relevant literature, and suddenly I discovered this wealth of new material which was, in effect, a renaissance of rhetorical studies, with researchers and thinkers in a variety of different geographic jurisdictions looking at the act of composing and the development of writing abilities and using a range of different disciplinary lenses. Ian and I began to fantasize about bringing together some of these thinkers and researchers, since many seemed to be just dimly aware of each other's work at that time, and then CCTE came along and gave us carte blanche to run a conference on writing. As I said before, preparing for this conference was itself a wonderful experience because, first, we got to invite the people who, from our reading, seemed to be developing brilliant new insights and, second, we got to read through the hundreds of proposals for papers, and then it became clear that something very important was happening across the English-speaking world, in terms of discovering and redefining a new discipline and a new psychic terrain. Ian and I named one of the books that emanated from the conference *Reinventing the Rhetorical Tradition,* and that is what we suddenly saw was happening: the reinvention of a tradition.

The smartest thing I did as a conference organizer was to hire someone to be responsible for all the administrative snafus during the conference itself so that I could attend all the sessions and be present at those wonderful presentations and especially at those extraordinarily lively exchanges from the floor after the presentations.

MARY: What was the most provocative encounter that stands out for you now?

AVIVA: Well, the session that stands out for me was the one where Janet Emig spoke about the tacit tradition. Her formulation of the twentieth century philosophic roots of this new discipline grounded and expanded the discipline for me in ways that continue to have relevance for me. And then, at the end, John Dixon rose to ask a question, about the classic and Scottish traditions of rhetoric, I believe, and the juxtaposition of the different traditions, as well as of the British and American perspectives. I got caught up in that one image, of the two of them, a Brit and an American, a man and a woman, one pointing to one tradition and the other to another, but together negotiating common ground and shared meanings. There were other wonderful encounters from the floor—Andrew Wilkinson and Lee Odell, Carl Bereiter and Andrew Wilkinson—and even more valuable, extended conversations over beer in the evenings and over lunch on those magically lovely days on the campus.

MARY: Looking back to the '78 and '86 conferences, do you think that we have made significant strides in the meantime?

AVIVA: Well, by '86, I think that the discipline was at a very different stage in its evolution. One thing that happened was that people had become far more aware of issues dividing us, which was the theme of the conference. The problem that concerned us, though, was that there was a tendency to gloss over these differences at conferences like the four C's, in a mistaken attempt, I believe, to be as supportive as possible. This sense that one ought to be as supportive and helpful as possible, even to the extent of glossing over important differences, was probably due to our fortress mentality in composition studies because we felt ourselves to be beleaguered by the literary establishment, in some ways, and by the public at large, in others. In fact, in organizing the conference, we kept getting confronted by very dramatic proof of the tendency to shy away from dealing with differences: very few people were prepared to engage in public scholarly debate. What especially concerned me, and still concerns me, is that the attitude behind this reluctance to debate issues was not just one of community solidarity, but also reflected a feeling that to attack an idea is to attack the person who holds that idea. I remember very vividly the answer given by one of our invitees, when they were invited to debate an issue with person X. Now the invitee was very critical of the assumptions behind X's research, but when asked to debate him, the answer was, "I couldn't possibly debate him, *he's such a nice guy."* We try, in our classes, to get kids to recognize that we hold ideas; we aren't those ideas, but we are the ones who need to be persuaded of that.

Ironically, very soon after that conference, we began to see divisions expressed and allegiances declared not just at conferences, but on the pages of leading journals. Unfortunately, though, there has been a lot of acrimony expressed, or not too well hidden, in these discussions. There's still too much personality and personhood attached to specific positions.

Looking at the Tension between Social Convention and Personal Invention

MARY: What are some of these major differences and issues that divide us?

AVIVA: Certainly in North America, there has been a clear division between those who take a cognitivist approach and those who see themselves as social constructivists. The cognitivists, and I'm thinking of Flower and Hayes, for example, or Bereiter and Scardamalia, have tended to look at writing as a cognitive activity engaged in by the individual, who develops as a result of internal maturation as well as appropriate learning experiences.

Research is typically more interventionist, like composing aloud, and contrived (often brilliantly so, as in the work of Bereiter and Scardamalia) to get at processes that are normally underground.

In contrast, the social constructivists tend to use ethnographic and naturalistic modes of inquiry because of their focus on the shaping powers of context. Like the Sapir-Worf hypothesis, there are extreme and modified versions of social constructivism. The extreme proponents like Richard Rorty, or in composition Ken Bruffee, argue that the self itself is a product of the constraining power of social and cultural forces. A more modified position is that of Charles Bazerman, who takes a more pragmatic, in the Jamesian sense, theoretic approach: he acknowledges an "I" that can make certain choices, but points to the enormous shaping power of the social and contextual forces that surround us from birth, and in particular as we try to construct knowledge in language.

MARY: What does this mean for teaching and teachers, especially with respect to the tension between social convention and personal invention?

AVIVA: There is a lot of incentive for teachers to opt for a cognitivist position, because it leads far more easily to specific teaching strategies. It's not a coincidence that Flower has come out with textbooks based on the Carnegie-Mellon work or that the Bereiter team published their own set of teaching strategies. Not only does the social constructivist position not translate easily into sets of portable strategies, it also places a great burden of responsibility on teachers because context is so important in shaping and constraining the way in which students know and engage with their worlds. Everything that happens in the classroom has potential impact, and so teachers become responsible not just for what they say and do, but also for what they don't say and don't do.

MARY: You are saying this depends on one's theoretic stance.

AVIVA: Yes. If you take a social constructivist perspective, then you will see that the degree to which you allow for or facilitate interactions in the classroom will make its impact on the directions in which students grow. One issue that I have been thinking about a lot, because of the kind of work I do here at the university, is related to writing across the curriculum. One very positive result of recent work in this area, in the sense of research into the kinds of things that are happening in different disciplines, has been or at least should be increased respect for what goes on in the disciplinary classroom. I realize that there has been a tendency by some English composition people to go into the disciplinary classrooms as missionaries, bringing them the "truth," trying to impose our values and practices onto their cultures. But the more I observe what goes on in disciplinary classes at Carleton University, the greater the respect I gain for what is actually happening there without our intervention. And the interesting thing is that what is going on is something that the disciplinary specialists themselves have no access to in terms of explicit description, because what is being conducted or constructed is often being conducted and constructed at a nonconscious level. The tacit dimensions of learning and teaching have yet to be fully acknowledged and explored.

The disciplinary teachers I have been observing go about setting up certain kinds of scaffolding by playing very subtle roles. For example, through the kinds of questions they frame in their assignments, they elicit from their students certain stances towards phenomena and certain ways of construing the phenomena with which they are presented. And these stances and these ways of construing experience are the interpretive stances of the disciplinary community. Over the year, the scaffolding provided by the professors becomes less substantial, and the students take more and more of an independent role in terms of thinking through issues in the ways in which the discipline expects its community members to be thinking. So the kind of initiation into disciplines is very subtle and nonconscious.

MARY: One of the things that most intrigued me in your study of law students learning to write within that discipline is the evidence you found that somehow they learned to write in the law register without being explicitly taught this register. If that is in fact the case, what implications does this have for the whole industry of freshman composition?

AVIVA: I have grave doubts about that whole industry, especially about the value of freshman composition as a means of teaching writing across the disciplines. There are certainly some useful things that can be done in freshman comp. For example, students may find journal writing a productive way to define for themselves their own roles with respect to society, to their family, to their peers, and to their culture. Personal writing, if we interpret it to mean that kind of writing that helps to navigate and chart an individual's own personal odyssey, can have a central role to play. However, we may very well ask whether every student should be asked to do this kind of writing and, if so, for what purpose.

MARY: Or we can ask: Does every student want to do this?

Learning and Writing across and within Disciplines

AVIVA: Wants to or needs to. Yes. I'm quite convinced that some people, who may be quite intellectual, don't discover their ideas through writing or through talk as much as I do, or maybe you do. Those of us who are teachers and those of us who are involved in this particular discipline have a vested interest in believing that discoveries are made through language. One thing that we have learned from Shirley Brice Heath's work is that there is more than one way. For example, language can be acquired in very different contexts, in ways that are very different from what was conventionally assumed to be THE WAY for learning language or eliciting the learning of language. Everything that we have learned from the studies of children of linguists about how they acquire language applies to children of linguists and perhaps to middle-class, English-speaking parents in general, but *not* necessarily to anyone else. We know that Einstein discovered his insights through no symbolic system, neither verbal nor mathematical, but through something akin to muscular imagery. I can see an optional writing course for students who would like to explore the worlds that they live in through language. I can even see a freshman composition course for students who would like to learn to write within the realm of public discourse. I'm thinking of pieces for newspapers or letters to politicians. And I suppose that I could even envision a kind of course that might be helpful for students in terms of learning to write for the disciplines, but this would be a very different course, one which would not fit neatly into the institutional structures set up by most universities. What you would want is to set up workshop formats for students to engage in the writing tasks set in other disciplines alongside other students engaged in those same tasks. The composition teacher would facilitate the workshops, would perhaps discuss possible strategies for invention and revision, but would not be responsible for setting or grading the assignments.

MARY: This seems to me like a tightrope walk between demonstrating to students this range of available strategies which they may or may not need or use and socializing of students into different academic disciplines, some of which may have institutionalized ways of behaving and expectations about what is appropriate or inappropriate. I guess what I'm getting at here is whether we encourage learning as an act of discovery or an act to fulfill the institutionalized expectations of academia. To put it more bluntly, are we reinforcing the "doing of school"?

AVIVA: Yes, that raises another very important distinction. Sometimes students themselves don't want to learn anything more than "doing school." Or less than doing school, for that matter, because our observations led us to marvel at what was entailed by doing school. Still, one of the interesting things we found with the law students is that, although they all ended up writing law papers which looked like law papers, we could differentiate the students according to the value they assigned the experience. For some students, writing the law essays was a valuable experience, and for others it was not. And one factor that accounted for this difference was the degree to which the assignment was challenging. If the assignment was too difficult, the students experienced anxiety. Some students found the task too easy. One kept complaining that the tasks were boring; she said that she preferred her political philosophy course work because the ideas were more abstract and the tasks consequently more challenging and fun. The interesting student was the one who redefined the task to make it more challenging for herself. This is a phenomenon that Bereiter and Scardamalia have described as taking the "high road," and it is something that the psychologists Csikszentmihalyi and Larson notice in their study of adolescents as well. But nobody seems to have the answer to the important pedagogic question: How can students be nudged towards reinterpreting the nature of tasks in order to make them more meaningful? How can we get them to do something more than simply satisfying the school task?

Looking at Oppositional Discourse and Varied Stances

MARY: I'm wondering if it isn't a personality issue. We talked earlier about the resistance among researchers at the '86 conference to engage in any kind of oppositional discourse. I think the same issue applies in classrooms. Is it an issue of power or personality or both?

AVIVA: Yes, individuality is one of a variety of factors. One of the things that we started to look at in the law study was ways to differentiate the varied stances of students. We like to talk about their "stances" rather than classify them as types, because the latter sounds as though there's a firmness and fixedness and that they can't move out of these positions. I don't think that's the case. I think that students do take different stances with respect to different experiences. For example, we were talking before about how some people find talk or writing a very effective heuristic and very useful as a way of exploring the world in general. Other people do not. It doesn't make necessarily better or more profound people, although it may mean that some stances may be more suitable for some kinds of tasks. That's all. But we did find certain preferences and situations where it made no sense to talk about ability. I remember very vividly one student who preferred to come back to the concrete and to think in terms of the concrete, whereas another, and these were both females which was interesting, preferred to think in terms of abstractions and she was aware of this preference. She was the one who liked the political philosophy class. Both students could consistently write abstractly and very effectively both in terms of their use of language and overall level of organization. It's just that, when given the choice, for example in their conversations with us, the one student preferred to talk and think in terms of abstractions, and the other always visualized in terms of the concrete. So we have very different stances, which are related to something other than ability.

MARY: Certainly what came out of my own study of middle grade French immersion children is the extent of the differences among the children in their stylistic preferences for writing stories in English and French, and about which they could talk very explicitly. The issue I see here is what implications does this notion of stylistic preference or stance preference have for that increased responsibility for the classroom teacher about which we talked earlier? How are teachers to respond to such diversity? Will some preferences be privileged over others, meaning that some voices will be heard and some will not?

AVIVA: Yes, it does come back to this tremendously increased responsibility for teachers, a responsibility to recognize the range of potential stances, and by that I mean something more than what people are calling "learning styles." Most of these categorizations seem to me to be quite trivial. The differences that my colleagues and I were seeing in our study were far more subtle and far more complex. Teachers are going to have to recognize this variation and the degree to which they may be, unintentionally, privileging some students and not others, or some kinds of learning over others. All this presents an enormous challenge. It also relates to your reference to oppositional discourse, which I'd like to pursue a little bit.

A number of times, I have raised with classes of teachers or intending teachers a point which James Britton has made about exploratory talk as opposed to argumentation. He says that the kind of loose exploratory talk that he has so many beautiful examples of in *Language and Learning* is the kind of talk in which people can move from their positions and in which real learning can take place. Whereas in an argument, where two people are opposed to each other, learning does not take place; each position just gets more entrenched. I have posed this distinction to classes to get their responses. Usually most agree, but in every class, there will be some people who will say something like the following: "Sure, it's true that in an argument I get more and more entrenched in my position, but I explore my position thoroughly, and I recognize that this is my role, to argue it through at the time. But afterwards, when I walk away, I take into account what the other person said so that my next argument will begin on very different grounds." I think that some people, for cultural or personal reasons, are very uncomfortable with oral arguments. Perhaps Britton is one of them. I suspect that that's the case; he's so gentle and gentlemanly as well. Other people are quite comfortable with arguments, like Janet Emig at both the '78 and '86 conferences. I think that she would say what some of my students are saying. They seem to be saying implicitly, "I'm taking a position, but the position is not me, and you can take the opposite position, and I know that it's not you. Let's see how far each position can be taken. Then afterwards, we can see where we want to go ourselves. In the meantime, let's push these positions as far as they can go." Notice that I have resisted saying that this may be a gender issue.

MARY: Typically people talk about females wanting to avoid confrontation and be good girls.

AVIVA: Yes, but I think that there's more to it. It's true that some females, maybe even most females, work towards developing and maintaining harmony. But the question of argument is more complex than that. Personally I can see an impulse within me which becomes alert and very uncomfortable at the least sign of disharmony within any social group where I find myself, but at the same time I am very comfortable with a set of assumptions guiding the group which say that it's okay to have an argument over issues or ideas. I suspect that that may be cultural. I grew up in a home where there were lots of arguments over issues, not over persons, but over issues. It was okay to criticize an idea that someone, *anyone,* expressed, but it was not okay to criticize any person in the family or at our table.

MARY: This whole issue of oppositional discourse and one's comfort zone within that mode is fascinating. I wonder how much of this willingness to engage in argument is a socialization issue, how much of it is related to personhood, our sense of selves as growing human beings. I find argument a very comfortable mode. I wonder how much of it is my training in English literature and linguistics. Linguists seem to be more comfortable with this mode, and I see a difference in the conferences I attend in academics' willingness to engage in a debate about ideas. What do you think?

AVIVA: I certainly do see differences in the different conferences that I attend. I was first struck by this at a conference on language testing in Israel that I attended a few years ago. The conference was sponsored by the British Council and attended by applied linguists primarily from across Europe and Israel. Actually, it was more a symposium than a conference. What struck me was the freedom with which the participants obviously felt to disagree with other presenters. It was so refreshing to go to a session, given by someone who was highly respected and very well liked by everyone present, where one person after another felt free to dissect the presentation, questioning the research paradigm, the methodology, the interpretation of the findings. And at the end, everyone, including the presenter, walked out smiling. The presenter clearly saw it as an opportunity to test out and refine ideas. This is not typical of a conference like the four C's. I'm not sure whether the difference is because of the difference in the disciplines or the cultures, but I've rarely seen this kind of frank and open dissection of another's views in their presence. And I really resent it when I hear more criticism in the halls than at the presentations.

MARY: Conferences can be cultures and discourse communities in and of themselves.

AVIVA: Yes, and you have to know how to read them, don't you?

MARY: Yes indeed. I think that the issue has important implications for teacher education and teachers in schools. I think of McDermott's notion of collusion: if you don't want to transform the school system, don't question; it just accommodates the status quo. If you don't engage in the ideas, you don't see a need to change or revise your ideas or reformulate your thinking.

AVIVA: That's right.

MARY: I started this conversation by talking nostalgically about the 1978 conference and how it changed my own thinking about issues. In 1990, perhaps, you might not like to entertain the thought of organizing another conference, but if you were to do so, what are some of the issues in which you would like participants to engage?

AVIVA: Well, I suppose there are two kinds of issues. One, and I have been thinking about this for a while, is to have a symposium on discipline-specific writing, including people from the sociology of science, to explore some basic issues relating to the social construction of knowledge in written discourse. I stress "symposium" because the model I have in mind grows out of that symposium I attended in Israel, in the sense that I'd like to see people come together as a working group, working towards the preparation of a set of papers, so that each person would orally present work-in-progress, and the responses of the other participants would enable that person to reshape and reformulate the ideas.

Another area relates to the whole issue of gender, which I know interests you too. Specifically I am interested in the way gender manifests itself in writing, that is, in the texts, in the processes, in the pedagogy. I intend to spend some time reappraising and reanalyzing some of my own research data from that perspective. I am not convinced that some of the models that are being presented do in fact refer to gender-specific patterns. Perhaps preferences or tendencies are more appropriate terms, and of course you must take into account culture and age and time.

MARY: Last year at four C's I was amazed to hear so many references in presentations to Belenky et al., *Women's Ways of Knowing,* a trendy topic right now.

AVIVA: It is a fine book, and it opens up whole new areas for exploration. But the fact that there is no comparable male group against which the women in the study are compared raises serious questions. I'd like to probe further. My hunch is that we will find preferences or tendencies by gender, and probably primarily, if not entirely, due to socialization, but I suspect we will also find independent cultural factors and important individual stylistic preferences. I envision a conference where people would come together in more interactive sessions to seriously probe and to play with these issues.

MARY: One final topic. How has the fact that you are a woman affected your thinking?

AVIVA: That's a good question, and one that I have only just recently begun to think about. Unfortunately, I was at the wrong place, both personally and geographically, when all the consciousness-raising sessions of the 70s were going on, and though I have undoubtedly benefited from all that thinking and the public policy it created, I am not cognizant enough of how. Clearly being a woman has affected my career, the years off to care for small children, the return to a devastated job market, the exploitation of my early professional years in Ottawa. It's a familiar story. But at the same time, there is a self-congratulatory voice in my head which keeps pointing out certain advantages to my position in the male-dominated world of the university. I like the marginality. Ironically, it was a male, Richard Young, who summed it up for me at a recent four C's when he talked about his own earlier marginalized position in rhetoric during the 60s before the discipline had been rediscovered. He quoted Loren Eiseley: "Life is most interesting at the margins." And he pointed out that when you live at the margins, you don't have to be successful, and you don't have to be respectable. And I do feel that positive absence, the absence of a need to be respectable and successful. I feel less pressure to play the "university game" than my male colleagues do. It's easier for me to take risks, I suspect, because I have less invested in what the onlookers might think. Does this make sense to you? I know that I have far less ego invested in my work than many of my male colleagues: slights don't affect me in the same way. I don't need a corner office.

But even as I say this, I have to acknowledge something else as well; I can feel the change taking place even as we speak, as they say. Because one of the terribly unfair things that has transpired in the last two decades is that the ante has been upped for women. We have been told that we are being permitted to have careers and professions, just like men, as long as we also continue to carry the traditional family responsibilities that our mothers and grandmothers carried. In fact, it isn't even an issue of "being permitted to have careers" for young women now: they are expected to have careers and to work at their careers with the same energy and single-mindedness as men with wives behind them, and at the same time they are expected to nurture their families with the same intensity and energy as women for whom this is their sole career. The situation is highly unfair, and I am afraid that the adrenaline that has been fueling us is about to run out. There have to be massive changes at the social level. But this is not an interview about women in society, although all this has powerful implications for women as teachers and researchers. Quite simply, we all need the time (not to speak of the psychic energy) to stand back and reflect on our practice if we are to develop as teachers and researchers and as human beings. And it is that time for reflection that women are currently being robbed of.

I'm sorry but I seem to have strayed, though, from the question you were asking. I think that you wanted to know about how being a woman affected my thinking and my stance as a researcher and teacher. It is hard to be introspective in that way, but my hunch about women I have known in general, including you, Mary, is that women tend to have more of what Keats called "negative capability," the ability to rest in uncertainty, to listen to the data without imposing abstract constructs too early, to listen to our students without categorizing them too quickly. Now, in fairness, we have to recognize that Keats was John and not Jane Keats. In other words, I think that this quality is gender related, rather than being gender specific. But I certainly see among researchers in our field, among female colleagues, and among my students who are women teachers this willingness to accept, to wait, to listen, to be receptive to cues and clues, and that's a quality that I see as feminine and feminist, and it's a quality that I would aspire to myself.

Resonating Themes and Points of Convergence

At the end of my interview (in its 1991 revised version), I refer to Keats's "negative capability" as a quality that distinguishes women's approach to teaching, to research, and to life in general. For Keats, negative capability connotes a paradoxical ability to lie fallow and be receptive, to remain open, trusting, and alert to experience, other ideas, and the simultaneous existence of contradictory notions. What is negative is the lack of ego, the lack of the insistent need to judge, to pigeonhole, to go for the structure at the expense of the texture.

This quality expresses itself again and again during all the interviews. There is throughout the insistence on the need to be open, to listen to our students, to listen to their parents, to listen to teachers. Repeatedly, Spencer, Gill, Emig, Dombey, and Rathgen argue against the imposition of top-down ideologies or institutional shackles. "One must allow and trust the response of any other to any experience."

One aspect of this negative capability is a repeated downplaying of self: not self-deprecation but something more positive. Spencer, for example, recognizes the fact of change, but deliberately refuses to take on the role of "prophet." In the same way, Emig gives homage to the second generation of scholars and points comfortably to her own shortcomings and gaps of knowledge. Indeed the format of the entire book is itself a striking instance of this negative capability. The fact that Mary chose to foreground others at her own expense is significant. And note her interviewing style: she provides precisely the right balance of support and redirection. She does very elegantly the kind of collaborative, supportive, conversational work that has been described in the literature as typically female.

Margaret Spencer opened a very fruitful line of inquiry when she placed in a historical context what it is we do with respect to literacy in our classes, forcing us thus to confront fundamental questions about why we do what we do. It is important to rediscover how people actually learned to read and write before school made it something they had to do. After all, this whole venture into mass education is a relatively recent phenomenon, and the initial strategies devised to deal with the problems of numbers in school are only one set of a possible range of strategies. Perhaps it is time to explore others. We all know how institutions codify and make rigid, and it may be time now to shake free of, or at least to reconsider, reassess, the particular set of codifications that we have been taught by the institutions to accept as immutable.

Margaret Spencer also insists that we reexamine the way we teach literacy by focusing on how literacy rays out beyond the classroom. She asks the question asked in another context by Charles Bazerman: "Where is the classroom?" At the same time, she urges us to reconceive what we do in the actual classroom in light of the out-of-school lives and goals, past, present, and future, of our learners.

The apprenticeship model that Margaret Spencer draws on in her discussion of reading is one that has particular resonance for me as I look at the kind of practice that seems most successful in writing. In essence, the teaching she envisions is based on the concepts of collaborative performance and scaffolding. It draws on notions such as the zone of proximal development and the internalization of social processes, derived from Vygotsky, and sees literacy as being acquired when the teacher and learner engage collaboratively to perform the same task; the attuned teacher gives over more and more of the task as the apprentice develops. There is considerable evidence in the literature on early language acquisition to confirm that this is what in fact happens in the home. Public literacy education has failed in this century, where it has been unable to invent strategies and to recognize occasions for allowing these collaborative interactions to continue to take place.

Mary's opening question referred to Janet Emig's address at the 1978 Learning to Write conference, an address that was later published as an essay entitled "The Tacit Tradition." I remember my excitement at hearing her presentation then, but I could hardly appreciate at that time the degree to which Emig's discussion would shape, focus, and anchor my own understanding of the discipline. In "The Tacit Tradition," Emig named those modern thinkers whom she called the forebears of the newly emerging discipline of rhetoric. In doing so, she not only contextualized the discipline, but more significantly, she formulated underlying notions about language, its relationship to experience, its relationship to knowing and learning, and the role of formal education in such learning. Throughout her career, Emig has displayed this knack for seeing through to basic issues, crystallizing for the discipline its sense of self, as well as defining new directions and possible lines of inquiry. She validated storying as a mode of knowing many years back and spoke out early against the hegemony of objectivist, positivist research paradigms.

I was struck here, as always in her work, by Emig's generosity, her quickness to see and respond to "other ways"—to historical studies as well as speculative, to narrative as well as exposition. She has had the courage to be feminine and feminist even in times when these approaches were considerably more marginalized. In this context, we should note the degree to which Emig allows us to go beyond sexual politics in order to define gender-related, rather than gender-specific, principles. The feminine she defines as follows: "One must allow and trust the response of any other to any experience." The female principle she defines is one that can characterize research as well as teaching, and that can be, and is, expressed by males as well as females.

May Sarton, in her autobiography, talks about how women learn to make do with, more accurately to make the most of, what we have on hand. When the man of the household—husband, father, or brother—brings home unexpected company, the woman of the house "makes up," invents, or creates a meal out of whatever is available in the pantry and refrigerator. I found in Henrietta Dombey's discussion a strong sense of precisely that ability to turn to one's advantage the constraints of a situation, be it national assessment, natural curriculum, or whatever. This is not Pollyanna speaking, though. She is keenly aware of how things can go awry. Recognizing this, however, she is fully prepared to capitalize on and reshape whatever circumstances offer in order to achieve something of independent value.

Consistent with this is her recognition of the need for constant adjustment and change. Education is a process of revising: "We can never get the English curriculum exactly right because it never stops moving, just as the English language never stops moving. And we must always be prepared to adjust it, to accommodate to change."

I like the tension in Dombey's discussion, her recognition of the need to maintain a careful balance between opening up to, indeed welcoming, the child's home and cultural environment, while at the same time recognizing that some environments are less enabling. In this way she acknowledges the school's responsibility to compensate for less enabling environments. She escapes the kind of cultural relativism that sometimes accompanies multicultural policies and that so often disadvantages children further.

I share Margaret Gill's concern to clarify what is a very basic misunderstanding of Donald Graves's work and of what people term the "Graves approach." Unfortunately, the misunderstanding is shared by both acolytes and detractors, and it is the acolytes themselves who sometimes give credibility to the attacks. If I understand Graves right, what is central to his discussions of pedagogy and research is a profound respect for and confidence in learners and teachers. He wants to empower students so that they become, in his analogy, landlords rather than tenants of their own writing and learning. He trusts them and expects them to live up to this trust by learning how to engage critically with the world. At the heart of this approach, I see the apprentice-master relationship, or the Vygotskian caregiver-child relationship, in which both collaboratively perform the task that the *student* intends, with the teacher providing only the scaffolding the student requires.

Such interactions need not be limited to "personal" writing as the detractors claim, although personal writing may be an appropriate mode for beginners. At the heart of the process approach is a faith in one-on-one interaction over unfolding text, with its concomitant belief in the enormous capacities of children as language learners and of adults as language teachers once they are given the power and the confidence to respond to their own intuitions. All this is accompanied by Vygotskian notions about internalizing what is played out in social interactions, about the role of intention, and about the uses to be made of scaffolding and sensitivity to the zone of proximal development.

Like Gill, I agree that it is naïve to argue that empirical, ethnographic research is first-level research. Ethnographic research asks different questions, uses different methods, and most significantly assumes a different reader, or at least a different kind of reading. The reader of ethnography needs to be more active, more engaged, more prepared to determine in what ways the situation described is similar to and in what ways different from hers. She needs to make the generalizations herself, to find out what can be extrapolated. Like literature, ethnographies are more than the abstractions or generalizations that can be lifted from them.

Significantly, Elody Rathgen uses the phrase "delicate balance" during her interview, and it is this term which characterizes her own stance throughout: a stance which allows her to define clear-cut educational goals and at the same time to acknowledge and respect both teacher and learner needs. Thus, in the national syllabus that she developed, educational goals are clearly established, while teachers are also given the freedom to "find their own space" within the syllabus. In a similar delicately maintained balance, Rathgen is able to define clear expectations for collaborative learning, while also insisting on the need to acknowledge and accept learners' and group preferences which may seem to run counter to these goals.

Throughout the interview, the tone that resonates is one of broad acceptance and trust, of the wise passiveness that listens attentively to those seemingly silent voices whose silence is so often misinterpreted. She takes the strong feminine stand that sees openness to diversity not as an indicator of weakness or capitulation, but rather as a sign of strength and an opportunity for growth.

I suppose it is natural for Canadians to idealize a country like Barbados, whose climate and beaches are evoked so insistently on the pages of travel brochures throughout our long, long winter. Patricia Symmonds's words, though, did little to dispel that idealized image from my mind. It is true that the issues she describes are familiar: the dominance of women in the teaching profession, the decline of out-of-school reading with the advent of television and video-games, the breakdown of the family. However, the cultural and personal energy and optimism that are heard in her interview are less familiar on this side of the Caribbean. On my own visit to Barbados a couple of years ago, I was very struck by a television commercial that I happened to catch. The advertisement was intended to encourage parents to read to their small children. The image selected was of a father cuddling and reading to his three- or four-year-old. The fact that such a commercial was aired suggested to me something of the clear-sightedness, the ability to define and solve problems, and the sense that all is possible, which are heard throughout Patricia's interview.

Selected Bibliography for Aviva Freedman

Reinventing the Rhetorical Tradition (co-edited with I. Pringle). 1980. Conway, Ark.: L & S Books.

Development in Story Writing. 1987. *Applied Psycholinguistics, 8,* 153–169.

Reconceiving Genre. 1989. *Texte, 8(9),* 279–292.

Show and Tell? The Role of Explicit Teaching in Learning New Genres. 1993. *Research in the Teaching of English, 27(3),* 222–251.

Wearing Suits to University: Simulating Genres and Simulation as Genre (co-authored with C. Adam and G. Smart). *Written Communication, 11,* 193–226.

Henrietta Dombey

I spoke with Henrietta Dombey in my hotel room in St. Louis in November 1989 on a cold, rainy evening. We both were attending the National Council of Teachers of English annual conference. Just prior to our taped conversation, we had attended an all-day IFTE executive meeting. Foremost on Henrietta's mind then was the Kingman Report and its impact on English teachers in England and ways to enable schools and families to respond intelligently. I have had many conversations with Henrietta since that memorable evening. I remember most vividly her visit to Montreal as a featured speaker for our 1989 language arts conference. During that week I was frantically trying to print my dissertation and was meeting with major obstacles with the laser printer in our faculty media center. Henrietta volunteered to pitch in and help. A true enabler indeed!

Between Then and Now

National Curriculum and Local Autonomy

MARY: It's a November evening, Henrietta, and here we are in St. Louis at the National Council of Teachers of English annual conference. Last April, Margaret Meek Spencer addressed our local language arts conference. At that time, I sensed that British educators have become increasingly concerned about the historical evolution of Mrs. Thatcher's conservative government intervention in and effects on the British school system. After hearing your talk this morning, I sensed that one of your concerns is what is happening in England at this very moment with respect to the National Curriculum and the Kingman Report.

HENRIETTA: Well, what is happening in England just now is fast-moving and colorful. We are in a situation where we are in the process of developing the content of our National Curriculum. The education act is now passed. This great Education Reform Bill, or the GERBIL as it is more commonly known, has many people in education very worried. One of the provisions is for a National Curriculum, something which is quite new, that is the organization of education on a countrywide basis. We have had a tradition of autonomy within our local educational authorities. That is, within the counties or cities, the schools and teachers have enjoyed a considerable degree of local autonomy in terms of what is studied and how it is studied, certainly until the two years that lead up to the first formal examinations at sixteen. So in the past we have enjoyed this local autonomy, which has meant that there have been some quite marked differences in the content of teaching in different parts of the country.

MARY: So you're saying that what's happening is that this whole tradition of local autonomy is being overturned in the interests of a National Curriculum, which suggests a pattern of uniformity in British schools.

HENRIETTA: Yes, most definitely a new pattern is being very rapidly imposed. We started off with some small movements in that direction, whereby local education authorities were obliged to develop countywide policies on a number of curriculum areas, but the National Curriculum takes that much further. The National Curriculum will lay down what has to be taught in terms of attainment targets, which are related to levels of attainment that most children will be expected to achieve at seven, nine, eleven, thirteen, and so on up the educational system. Those attainment targets are presented in traditionally conceived curriculum areas. For example, there is a curriculum with its own set of attainment targets in math, another one in science, another one just recently published in English. There will be in the future attainment targets for history, for geography, and so on covering these traditional subject areas of the curriculum. The notion of a centrally devised curriculum is something that is quite new to us and that we have found really difficult to accommodate. However, the paradox is that, in the curriculum areas that have thus far received attention, the documents that have resulted, although they have been produced by the working parties set up by the Secretary of State, do *not* represent a repressive return to discredited practices, but do represent instead a kind of codification and articulation of something that we say with good conscience is like the best practice that we have seen.

Professional Development, Levels of Attainment, and Tests

MARY: This notion of levels of achievement or attainment is very interesting. I think in Canada we have always looked to England as being very forward-looking in terms of children's language and learning, and certainly have drawn on your language theorists like Britton, Dixon, and Meek for some of our own provincial curriculum documents. Within current developmental theory, the whole-levels notion and stage theory are being questioned. What will the levels notion mean to teaching and learning in British schools? What will this mean to British language and learning theory?

HENRIETTA: Well, of course there are and must be grave underlying doubts about any system that implies a levels notion. This is especially true for language learning. Certainly we question the idea that language is learned in a strictly linear fashion with a preordained route that every child will follow so that any child can be assessed in terms of how far he or she is along that route. I think we can see certain lines of development in terms of simple competencies to more complex competencies, relative inexperience to relative experience, a relatively narrow range of competencies to a broader range of competencies. But inevitably any attempt to codify those in terms of levels is going to be crude. However, it seems that such a system of levels of attainment has the potential for being less distorting than norm- or criterion-referenced testing.

MARY: How do you see an evaluation system changing or influencing teacher practice? You seem to be hinting at this.

HENRIETTA: I would think that an evaluation system, in the eyes of many teachers, in the eyes of their pupils, and in the eyes of the parents of those students, can dignify much valuable learning that is going on at present and could give it a public significance that at present it may lack. For example, in the area of reading, most of the assessment that goes on in our primary schools in most areas is of a very crude sort. It assesses children's capacity first of all to decode a list of disconnected words, or to complete in a conventional way incomplete sentences, or to insert again conventionally acceptable words in a cloze procedure exercise. In other words, it expects children to deal with short, decontextualized passages or sentences, or even individual words, and not to engage with print in the context of a larger purpose, not to invest the print with any personal significance, or take from it anything that relates to any occupation they're engaged in. The public significance such belittling assessment is accorded demeans the valuable work that goes on in many classrooms.

I hope that the attempt is going to be made in the assessment of the National Curriculum to reflect children's ability to read in a way that relates what they read to their own experience, to read in different styles for different purposes, to read with discrimination, to reread, and talk about what has significance, to develop favorites, to know how to choose, to know how to find relevant material for study purposes, and so on. All those aspects of reading, all those vital lessons, we know will enable children to become better students, to become more participatory citizens, to gain sustenance from the written word, to gain autonomy through the written word. All those kinds of important reading lessons we hope, and I think the hope isn't a totally vain one, will be recognized and thereby dignified by the new assessment procedure.

MARY: I'd like to pick up on your feeling of hope. You have been here in North America for a few days and have probably heard a lot more pessimistic messages about evaluation, assessment, and schooling on this side of the ocean. I am thinking right now of Shirley Brice Heath's keynote address this afternoon, "Will Schools Survive?" How do you see school systems, not just those in Britain, but all school systems in this vast technological world, being able to deal with the kinds of things you've just said, which are very nice, very idealistic. But how can we realistically do this?

HENRIETTA: Well it's already happening, isn't it? We know that in your country, and in my country, there are classes where children do engage in reading for a wide variety of valid purposes, whose significances they recognize themselves. We know that's already happening. What I'm saying is that an attempt to codify those important and significant lessons in a National Curriculum and to assess them must dignify these lessons and enable others outside the classroom to see their importance. Well, an attempt can potentially do that. But there is of course the possibility, and I think you're very right in hinting at it, that we won't get it right. There's the possibility that the assessment procedures will not reflect the attainment targets, and will not reflect the intentions of those who drafted what is at the moment only a consultation document.

There's also the danger that the less confident teacher or the teacher who is firmly entrenched in practices based on a narrower conception of what reading and writing and talk are about might try to treat the curriculum documents as a syllabus, to teach new lessons in old ways and thereby experience only dissatisfaction and anxiety and pass on much of that to the children in his or her charge. So I see this as a grave danger, and I see it as also indicating that we need very extensive inservice, extensive both in terms of its spread and extensive in terms of the time that's devoted to it. You have a good model with your own inservice work in Montreal. I see we need inservice courses of different sorts, many of them based in the schools if we are to give teachers the confidence to hold on to what they have that is good and to develop new ways that are productive and relate to the National Curriculum.

MARY: What is your ideal version of inservice in contrast to the reality of what you see right now?

HENRIETTA: Well, the model that finds most favor in official circles at home is known as the cascade model. Now I for one find that term rather inappropriate. "Cascade" suggests to me something flowing and flowering, the sun glinting through beautiful drifting spray. Well, that's not what it's like at all. "Cascade" is a term that's used for a mass injection program, because it's a program that happens in stages. One lot injects the first tier, the first tier injects the second tier, the second turns around and injects the third tier and so on. And it's based on a transmission model of teaching. It is based on short, small, sharp, concentrated doses, and this has very little place for any articulation of the concerns of those on the receiving end and very little opportunity for them to shape the experience themselves.

The kind of thing that would be much more productive would be if schools could give teachers more opportunity, with some assistance from the outside, to explore their own curriculum, to explore their own strengths, to relate what they do to the demands of the National Curriculum, to tentatively try out ways of expanding and extending what they do that will accommodate the demands of the National Curriculum without losing sight of what they regard as valuable and enduring in their existing ways of organizing their teaching and carrying it out.

MARY: What do you see as the most important thing that teachers need to know about organizing their teaching then? I don't mean just in Britain. Are there some general principles? Some general insights you would like to share from, or even take back to, Britain?

HENRIETTA: I feel one of the things I'd like to take back is the three-hour session on assessment yesterday, where there was just a tremendous spirit and determination amongst the teachers that their work should not be distorted or misrepresented by inappropriate assessments. And they were very unawed by the Commissioner for Education for Missouri. There were a number of Missouri teachers there who were ready to argue back about the inadequacy, as they saw it, of the current testing going on. It sounded as if they had a pretty good knowledge of the testing arrangements and how they failed to reflect either the valuable processes the children engaged in in the classroom or the demands of the outside world. So what I want to take back is that sense of determination of those teachers working in a situation which is far more test bound, far more constrained by tests of all different sorts. The impression that we tend to have at home is that there are tests all the time in most parts of the United States. We know that there are end-of-section tests, end-of-term tests, and so on. We know about all this machine scoring, but somehow we tend to have the impression that most teachers are perfectly happy about it and go along with it. And we're rather patronizing about American teachers. What I want to take back is that that patronizing attitude is quite misplaced, that the American teachers I encountered at this conference have a very clear, intelligent, perceptive, and well-informed idea of what they could and should be doing in their classrooms, and they feel enormously frustrated when they have to work to these tests.

MARY: Do you think the situation of these American teachers is vastly different from that of the teachers you work with in Brighton?

HENRIETTA: Yes, I think it is rather different because for the moment our teachers work with fewer tests. The tests don't penetrate so far into the curriculum. There may be reading tests, but there aren't writing tests. I think the constraints are rather more subtle at home. However, the tests that we do have lay emphasis on certain less exacting, less exciting, less enlarging, less enabling aspects of teaching and learning. But those tests that we do have don't reach as far, aren't administered as frequently, and may be rather more subtle and complex than most of the tests that the people in yesterday's session were enduring and chafing about.

MARY: Do you think that the National Curriculum will eventually have more teachers chafing in England than here?

HENRIETTA: I think it does depend; I mean I think I was overenthusiastic in the early part of what I've said to you and I might now want to moderate that in some way. What I do want to emphasize is that the effect of the National Curriculum, whether it is by and large a good effect or by and large a constricting and limiting effect, will depend crucially on two things. And the first is the form of the assessment. The second is the form of the inservice support that teachers are given.

   If things go wrong, if the assessment instruments fail to reflect the attainment targets as laid out in the current documents, fail to reflect the conception of teaching that is included in the language and literacy framework, then that document will to that extent be fictionalized and marginalized. The assessment will determine whether those brave words actually do herald a further spread, a dissemination of good practice, or whether they represent a diminishing, a belittling of what is best practice.

MARY: You have been talking about best practice. Do you see a dichotomy between preservice and inservice teachers' teaching practices?

HENRIETTA: I think that it depends very much where you are. There are some forward-looking, alert, and lively institutions for initial teacher education, some of which are located in areas where there isn't much leadership and teachers don't have much support for developing a classroom practice or theory of learning. So you get students who have a desire, for example, to emphasize the process in writing, to work in a workshop way with children in school, to understand developmental writing, and so on. They go into classrooms where this is treated with hostility and where the students' lack of experience is pounced on in order to discredit the style of teaching that they're trying to engage in. But you get the converse of that too. You get educational authorities where the teachers are supported by exciting inservice, where they collaborate together and develop with practice and support each other, and move forward in ways that are exciting to see, but the institutions of initial teacher education are dull, unexciting, and peddling ideas that have long since failed to prove themselves. These are two dichotomous situations. One thing that might result from the codification of best practice in the National Curriculum is that a student teacher and a classroom teacher would be working at least nominally towards the same attainment target.

MARY: That makes a lot of sense. How can we work towards more coherent teacher education programs?

HENRIETTA: Well, this is a challenging problem. What it means is that nominally the regular classroom teacher and the student who is doing his or her teaching practice might be working towards the same attainment targets, but they might construe them very differently, and they might have a very different conception of the best route towards those attainment targets. So the existence of a National Curriculum is no guarantee against some kind of conflict, some continuation of the sorts of conflict that frequently exist at the moment between the kinds of practices the students try to engage in and what the teacher is normally trying to do with a task or the class.

MARY: Are you suggesting there will always be this kind of tension between these two groups of teachers?

HENRIETTA: Tell me if I've got it wrong. I don't think there is always a tension between what's going on in the regular classroom and the institution of teacher education. I'm saying that there are situations where that does exist and that the existence of a National Curriculum might go some way towards mitigating that. But it can't do the whole thing. I mean I think we have to do far more on the human level.

MARY: Perhaps this is the area which presents the biggest challenge, as institutions are not always the most humane contexts for learning.

HENRIETTA: Yes, I think that we need to make teacher training more of a collaborative enterprise between the institutions of higher education and the schools themselves. And I think we need to do more than we are at present, in the way of bringing teachers into teacher education institutions and having the professors go into the schools and teach. There needs to be far more interpenetration of the institutions and far more sharing. If that were the case, then I think the possibility of harmony would grow.

Enabling Schools and Enabling Families

MARY: You make me think of other harmonies, that is, more harmonies between not only teacher education institutions and schools, but between homes and schools, communities and schools, especially in light of our multicultural world.

HENRIETTA: Yes, the home and school relationship is an extremely interesting area. That's one theme in which I think nothing has definitely been developed at this convention. I think we've learnt over the last few years to be much more respectful of the learning that goes on in the homes. We've learnt to be more respectful, particularly through the work of Barbara Tizard and Martin Hughes on young children learning at home and in school. They have shown us that children's talk at home, even in the most modest homes, is more wide ranging, more complex, more sustained than the talk in most school classrooms. We have learnt from other sources that the home is a place of very potent and very powerful learning. We need to somehow extend that and extend our conception of what learning to be a full, adult member of the community is all about, so that we can see that what goes on in school is only a relatively small part of that. And the more we can understand the nature of the larger enterprise, the more we can adapt and modify and extend what we do into school to make a better fit. And that means of course understanding that the dynamics of different families, of different social groups, of different ethnic groups do vary very greatly. It means that we need to learn to accommodate many different dynamics, many different conceptions of roles of school learning, of the nature of the school learning, and so on. We need to accommodate them all without necessarily succumbing to them, because some of those conceptions may actually be limiting to the individual children concerned. So we need to recognize and respect them on the one hand, but not to be totally limited by them; I see this as a very complex problem.

MARY: It is a complex problem. I think that the ethnographic studies of how young children are socialized into and experience reading and writing in different cultural contexts makes E. D. Hirsch and his cultural literacy movement—the predetermined, prepackaged canon of codified knowledge every American should know—look pale and pathetic.

HENRIETTA: Yes, we need to change our old ways of dealing with home and school. I think of times when teachers have gone into children's homes as missionaries to say this is how you do it. I think we've got to be much more prepared to learn. I think of situations where teachers have invited parents into school, and they've invited them in as helpers, as audience, as lesser beings, to witness something of the miracle that is formal education. This is a slight overdrawing of the picture, but I think that we have to recognize that we need to invite parents into school in a different spirit. We have to visit their homes in a different spirit, and we have to invite parents in to contribute not just in the image of what the teacher does, but to share something of their own expertise, their own conception of what education is about, and their own versions of literacy and so on. In this way we can make the school more of a marketplace, if you like, and less of a chain store.

MARY: That's an interesting metaphor. I live in North America and your metaphor makes me think of the comment by literary critic Roland Barthes, which goes something like this: The goal of a literary education is not to make the child a consumer of stories but a producer of stories.

HENRIETTA: Yes, I agree.

MARY: And I want to connect this statement to your own work in which you show so well how children are producers of stories.

HENRIETTA: This is why I was rather cautious about the notion that we might become locked into the present culture of the family, because I'm not sure that all families enable children to develop as producers of stories, as initiators of conversation, as determiners of their own agendas, and so on. And it seems to me that Wells has shown us that this is what the families do where children's language develops most rapidly, most productively. Such enabling families behave in those ways. But we have in the past not been eminently successful in doing that in school. I was interested in my own research with nursery school children to work with teachers that seemed to be successful in initiating children who came from homes where literacy played little part, into an active and competent literacy. It seemed that almost on a semi-intuitive basis the teacher was modeling her classroom interactions on those kinds of productive, enabling interactions that Wells and Tizard and Hughes have documented in the enabling homes.

MARY: Let's pursue this role of enablers and your suggestion that we're living in a society where we cannot guarantee that the familial situation is going to be an enabling situation. We are already seeing that we have children from different cultural backgrounds coming to school with very different expectations of the culture of schooling and the culture of childhood.

HENRIETTA: I don't think this is necessarily anything new. I think that the rigid, paternalistic Victorian family was not necessarily always enabling.

MARY: That's true and there is still quite a residue of this attitude at all levels of our educational and societal institutions.

HENRIETTA: I think that certain public rhetoric invests such traditional families with virtues that they did not always display.

MARY: What you're saying then is that we've always had, both in our society and in our educational system, a dichotomy between the real self and the presentational self, the authentic and nonauthentic, a double standard so to speak.

HENRIETTA: Yes, but I am more concerned with the notion of "the democracy versus the autocracy." The enabling family seems to be essentially a democratic family where children's voices count, where what they say is taken notice of, not just in terms of all the niceties, but in terms of substance.

MARY: It all depends on how we look at children.

HENRIETTA: Yes. Yet we all know that, now in some degrees and in the past perhaps to a greater degree, there are families that are very autocratic and hierarchical, where children's words and experiences do not count.

MARY: I agree. And I guess what I was thinking of is how people present themselves, reveal themselves by their language and behavior, which can be in the person-persona of controller and manipulator or liberator and dialoguer. What I mean is that there are those that would be much more inclined to feed into an autocracy to please someone else, to get on with what they have to get on with. I think your democracy versus autocracy notion relates to what happens in a classroom in terms of Irving Goffman's notion of presentation of self. Are there some children who are more inclined to be teacher pleasers? I am talking about those children and even adults who are much more willing to play at the game of school than to express their ideas and expose their true selves.

HENRIETTA: Right, right and who are less concerned about articulating their own ideas and expressing themselves than with feeding into and playing out what others want.

MARY: Or playing out what society seems to want or demand.

HENRIETTA: Or playing along with what the teacher wants.

MARY: Or playing along with what the teacher educator wants or the researcher wants.

HENRIETTA: Filling the bill that somebody else has decided and predetermined. I think that is a very real concern. If we think that education is anything like an intellectual endeavor, we must worry about such matters.

MARY: And how do we deal with that?

HENRIETTA: I don't know how we deal with that. We have to make people feel at ease; we have to make people feel at home. I mean, insecure people tend more to be anxious to please than to honestly express their ideas. We have to make people feel confident and valued, and feel that their views count.

MARY: How can we do that in the educational system, especially at the tertiary level, which we were talking about a little earlier? I see too many of our students wanting to "do school," and I am concerned about those individuals because they're going to be working with children.

HENRIETTA: I think that a lot of our students also tend to come in with that frame of mind. They want to be primary school teachers for a number of complex reasons, some to do with playing school and some to do with some kind of exercise of power. They are both different sides of the same coin.

MARY: The double-sided coin. Hmm, this makes for a complex exchange of currency in the educational enterprise.

HENRIETTA: Yes. I think giving them experience of working collaboratively in college is important, and giving them an understanding of children is important. They need to see that children are not powerless individuals waiting to be energized by being given the information and the skills by a teacher. But if and when student teachers develop some understanding of the strength of children's autonomous learning and the potential of that learning, they gain a respect for that. If they know something of, and if they appreciate something of the dynamics of children's learning, if they appreciate also something of the power of the discourse into which the children are being initiated, whether it's mathematics or science or whatever, then those two things together, I think, help protect them against a kind of accepting role, a kind of hierarchical conception and so on that we have been talking about.

I'm thinking in particular of a language course I teach. Just recently I've asked the third-year students who have elected to do a study of language development to take a four-year-old child and with a considerable amount of classroom observation to make some analysis of the linguistic systems the child has mastered and the uses to which these systems are put. And in every case the student has struggled long and hard and found the transcription and analysis initially difficult. But in every case at the end of the analysis they say such things as, "It's extraordinary what this child can do; just look how in a range of two minutes she is manipulating me, she is leading the conversation, she is informing me, she is persuading, she is thinking something through, she is using this variety of structures, and so on." And they gain a tremendous respect for children's language learning, for the learning that children have undertaken before they have even entered a formal institution. That kind of respect is a good start, although it's not enough, contributing very usefully to protecting the students against a blind, accepting role.

MARY: I'd like to pick up on the blind and accepting position. I think you would agree that we've heard a lot in the last number of years about collaborative learning and collaboration in classrooms. Is there a danger that there are some children, teachers or even researchers for that matter, who will in a collaborative situation be just blind and accepting and just let the group carry it all? I've seen that happen in a number of situations.

HENRIETTA: I've seen it happen also, and I think it's very important that children are given experiences of collaborative activity which demand participation and which don't allow individuals to be carried, and which don't allow individuals to dominate. That takes some devising and ingenuity. Initially dramatic activities and role play activities and so on can make it difficult for one partner to be carried. I think it's something that is a constant danger in every human enterprise. You could say that this afternoon we were engaged collaboratively in refining a document we had in front of us. [This is a reference to a revision of the constitution at a business meeting of the International Federation for the Teaching of English.] Some of us switched in for a bit and switched out for a bit; some people participated more, and some people participated less but more usefully and incisively. I think it's unrealistic to expect a uniform quality of participation in any group. I would say today we had a group of very interesting people. The discussion was good and we got somewhere. We got something done, and what was significant was that we all had a stake in it. And if it's a task that all could have a stake in, then those who are quiet, I would hope, are quiet because they genuinely are quiet or happy with what's going on and not because they can't be bothered or they appear bored or what have you. But I do think it's unrealistic to expect uniformity; personality differences, socialization differences, and so on will mean that people have different styles.

MARY: So what you're implying is how we can accommodate and celebrate the diversity that we encounter in a group situation rather than producing silent, accepting clones.

HENRIETTA: I think that is something we need to do and something we need to think a lot more about, especially how we can capitalize on this diversity.

MARY: Rather than viewing it as a problem.

HENRIETTA: Or rather than even making it into a problem.

MARY: Is there anything else you want to share in this interview either about what's happening in England or your experience here.

HENRIETTA: I may have been too enthusiastic about our curriculum document at the beginning. The notion of a written curriculum is something which is very new to us. We're fearful that National Curriculum will take a very repressive form. When we see that it doesn't, I think perhaps there's a danger as well that we welcome it too strongly and that we're insufficiently aware of the fact that it's relatively easy to produce an acceptable document, but it is considerably harder to extend and develop practice in schools in productive ways. And though the document and the associated assessment instruments may help us towards that, they can never provide particulars.

MARY: What you're saying is really that when it comes to teaching and learning and curriculum change we shouldn't sit too comfortably with our assumptions.

HENRIETTA: Well there're two things. One, that you don't just change people through nice documents and assessment instruments. The other is that we can never get the English curriculum exactly right because it never stops moving, just as the English language never stops moving. And we must always be prepared to adjust it, to accommodate to change.

Assessment and England's National Curriculum: What It Looks Like in Autumn 1991

Several years ago, I sat with Mary Maguire and vacillated between optimism and pessimism over the dramatic changes in the English school system that were then just moving towards the *Statute Book* of our Houses of Parliament. The optimism seemed at that time to be in the ascendant: despite an undertow of doubt, I felt enormously heartened by the proposals for primary English published only a few days earlier. Many shared my positive reaction, not least the educators from all over the English-speaking world who scrutinized the primary English proposals in a workshop session at the St. Louis NCTE convention, where Mary interviewed me.

Back in England these proposals were warmly welcomed by classroom teachers, head teachers, advisers, and those like myself involved in teacher training. In the "Programmes of Study," thoughtful innovators saw descriptions that would accommodate and even encourage the practices they held to be most productive. In the "Statements of Attainment," they saw a brave attempt to set out, in the ten-level framework common to all National Curriculum subjects, significant achievements in the learning of English. We were all encouraged to see, for example, that at level 3 (the level of the average nine-year-old or the able seven-year-old) children should be able to "demonstrate, in talking about stories and poems that they are beginning to use inference, deduction and previous reading experience to find and appreciate meanings beyond the literal."

But many were worried, as I was, about how teachers would be helped to interpret this curriculum and make it live for their children. And the concerns about assessment that I'd expressed to Mary were widely shared. Many of us doubted whether any centrally devised instrument could assess with any validity a curriculum as broad and as imaginatively conceived as the curriculum for Key Stage One that was inscribed on our *Statute Book.* As we looked through the "Statements of Attainment," it seemed that many would be hard to assess formally. Statements requiring children to read labels and notices in their normal environment and to demonstrate their knowledge of the alphabet in their use of word books or dictionaries posed problems. Even more problematic in assessment terms were the level-2 statements requiring children to "read a *range* of material with some independence, fluency, accuracy and understanding" (my emphasis).

Such matters, we were told, would be the province of teacher assessment; that is, they would come from teachers' own informal observations carried out in the normal course of events. But yet teachers were given no clear format for recording this teacher assessment or any clear guidance on how to carry it out. We suspected it was not being taken seriously and was only included as a sop to teachers' professional concerns. And then in 1990 we were told that, where the result of teacher assessment was in conflict with the result of the formal Standard Assessment Task (SAT), the SAT result would be preferred. So the more readily measurable elements of the curriculum were insidiously gaining an ascendancy over the others.

A vast amount of expensive work went into preparing these SATs for the seven-year-old age group. There was an honest, if not always enlightened, attempt to cover as much of the curriculum as possible within the constraints of a uniform assessment instrument. The resulting SATs were tried out on a small scale in the summer of 1990, and with all children in the age group the following summer. The results are just being published as I write.

The mood is now very different from the optimism of three years ago. Teachers' sneaking doubts and suspicions have hardened into bitter disillusion. Far from having a varied, valid, and informative assessment of a lively curriculum, we have a rather limited program of testing, set to get narrower still. Its results are presented and interpreted not in a way that helps the nation appreciate what children in this age group have achieved and how we could improve this. Instead, they are used as another stick to beat teachers with.

In the local and national press, on radio and TV, screaming headlines berate teachers for test results that show some 28 percent of the nation's seven- (or nearly seven-) year-olds to be below the expected level for their age group in reading. That the figures show a normal spread, with 21 percent above the level expected, excites no comment. There is no mention of the many statements of attainment that have to be satisfied, or of the broad and challenging conception of reading which informs them. And of course, as many of us feared, there is no mention at all of the teacher assessment.

While the tests inevitably failed to assess the full range of the English curriculum, they were not as narrow as they might have been. Where reading was concerned, they involved teachers assessing children's observations on stories read aloud to them, as well as their accuracy, fluency, and understanding in reading a passage from a children's book on an approved list. As are all searching tests of young children, the reading test was fairly time consuming, needing some twenty minutes of the teacher's undivided attention for each child.

Before the results were published, with no public discussion and in blithe disregard for professional opinion, Mr. Clarke, the abrasive Secretary of State for Education, decided that this reading test should be "streamlined." So the response to the story read aloud has been dropped. But the changes don't stop there. In order to achieve discrimination within the broad band of level 2, where, as expected, most children had been placed, he also decided to add a further element, a test of word recognition. So word recognition, which on the *Statute Book* appears as one aspect of the complex competence that is reading, has now been singled out and made to stand proxy for the whole.

The reading curriculum still stands in its full glory on the *Statute Book*. It is still fully taught in many primary schools, those where teachers' inner professional convictions tell them that their pupils deserve nothing less. But the more timid, the less experienced, and those whose strengths lie in other curriculum areas are already weakening. They see the writing on the wall. They see that it is word recognition that matters now, not responses to stories read aloud or the range of books children can read and understand. They fear the pillory of the local press.

What is happening in reading at Key Stage One has its counterparts at other key stages and in other curriculum areas. Following a whim of our Prime Minister expressed in a speech in July, course work is to be drastically reduced in assessment in all subjects at Key Stage Four. The brief for Key Stage Three has been savagely revised in line with this. Terminal examination is the watchword, spelling destruction for staged assessment, for breadth, depth, and range. The authenticity of the real is rejected in favor of the contrived. This is done in the name of Standards, Rigor, and The Basics. Everywhere there is a de facto reduction of the curriculum to what is easily and cheaply assessable, in the name of these three undefined virtues.

Meanwhile the business of assessing and reporting on the performance of schools and the education service as a whole is undergoing a similar reductive process. Simple "results" are to hold sway. Schools are to be compelled by law to publish and be judged on the raw figures of pupils' SAT scores, taking no account of the social factors influencing these.

And Her Majesty's Inspectorate (HMI), an institution that has performed with considerable expertise, independence of judgment, and devotion to duty the tasks of reporting to schools on the effectiveness of their teaching and to the government on the state of the education service, is now to have its numbers drastically cut and its brief restricted to training (in one week), licensing, and supervising teams of private "inspectors" who will compete in the marketplace to sell inspection services to schools. Who will have the important duty of reporting to government on the effectiveness of their reforms is far from clear.

The Assessment of Performance Unit, a governmental agency set up in the wake of the Bullock Report on reading and language some fifteen years ago, has operated on the basis of selective monitoring through tests more subtle, varied, and wide-ranging than any can be that have to be administered to entire populations. Over the last ten years, it has produced enormously useful information on patterns of attainment in science, mathematics, and English, showing performance in English to be in general improving, not falling as the government would have us believe. But its latest science report was suppressed, and the unit has now been disbanded. The SATs, we are told, will tell us all we need to know. Meanwhile the possibilities of large-scale evaluative research being carried out by universities or other bodies relatively independent of the government are receding to vanishing point as the funding for such work becomes ever more problematic. The assessment of individual children, of schools, and of the educational system as a whole will in no way match up to the demands of the National Curriculum.

The other sneaking fear I confessed to Mary concerned inservice support. There is little to say about this. Institutions of higher education are drastically reducing the scope and size of the courses they offer as teachers have neither the time nor the financial support to follow anything substantial. Yesterday I reported to the appropriate board of my polytechnic that a diploma course in language literacy and learning, which had run successfully for many years and won plaudits from teachers, HMI, and many others, was no longer viable. Instead, we are offering a series of courses which are briefer and more superficial.

Every month there is less and less provided by local education authorities, as the government reduces their sources of revenue while increasing the demands made on them. Unsurprisingly, but unusual for a period of recession, teachers are leaving the profession in large numbers, unable to endure being blamed for a fall in standards repeatedly trumpeted but never proved, being reviled for their professionalism as if this were nothing more than the protectionism of a self-perpetuating clique, and being prevented from developing the more thoughtful and informed practice they know will benefit their children and give them greater satisfaction.

We still have a good curriculum in English on the *Statute Book,* but we fear that the next move will be to cut it down to the size of what is being assessed.

Selected Bibliography for Henrietta Dombey

Learning the Language of Books. 1983. In *Opening Moves: Work in Progress in the Study of Children's Language Development,* edited by M. Meek, 26–43. Bedford Way Papers 17. London: Institute of Education, University of London.

Stories at Home and at School. 1988. In *The Word for Teaching Is Learning: Language and Learning Today: Essays for James Britton,* edited by M. Lightfoot and N. Martin, 70–81. London: Heinemann; Portsmouth, N.H.: Boynton Cook.

The SATable and the unSATable: Giving Our Children the Assessment in Literacy They Deserve. 1991. In *Celebrating Literacy, Defending Literacy,* edited by C. Harrisson and E. Ashworth. London: UKRA and Basil Blackwell.

Words and Worlds: Reading in the Early Years of School. 1992. Published jointly by the National Association for the Teaching of English and The National Association of Advisers in English.

First Steps Together: Early Literacy in European Contexts (co-edited with M. Meek Spencer). 1994. London: Trentham Books.

Elody Rathgen

I first met Elody Rathgen at the IFTE conference in Ottawa in 1986. I introduced her at a paper session on gender bias and the English curriculum. We both had forgotten about this earlier occasion, as readers will note by my remark which opens our conversation. There were two subsequent occasions for us to connect and converse: the 1987 conference in East Lansing, Michigan, and the 1989 NATE national conference held in Swansea, Wales, when she became president-elect of IFTE. Our conversation in this book took place in April of 1991 at the Montreal Convention Centre. Elody was a guest speaker at this national conference of the Canadian Council of Teachers of English, which was hosted by our local professional association. She was also IFTE's representative. I sense an ironic twist in Montreal as actual locale for our conversation about living between languages and cultures.

Listening to Different Voices and Silent Voices

MARY: I'm thinking back to the first time we met. It was at the IFTE conference in East Lansing.

ELODY: Yes.

MARY: Speaking of conferences. You had some part to play in the recent IFTE conference, "Different Voices," in Auckland, New Zealand.

ELODY: It was an interesting event and much smaller than other conferences such as the Ottawa one or an NCTE conference. Being smaller made it perhaps more intimate. People remember seeing each other there and talking with one another. It was a conference that put people personally on the spot because they were asked to do something about the theme of "Different Voices." You could not have gone through the conference without having heard different voices and having to make decisions. For example, if an issue came up, you had to ask yourself: Am I going to do something about it or quietly pretend it hasn't happened? So there was this nice sense of intimacy. It wasn't always comfortable for some people. I think there would be many who would agree that they were pushed to limits and forced to reconsider issues: Am I going to accept different students' voices or am I going to take a bit of their voice away from them and give them some of the voice I am more comfortable with? What about different Englishes in the classroom? People who had difficulty with these issues included many New Zealanders as well, even though we have done a lot of work and made claims about their sensitivity to race, particularly Maori culture and gender.

MARY: I remember these issues came up at the IFTE conference in Ottawa, but I felt then that people were trying to shy away from the issues. Do you think people confronted the issues at the Auckland conference?

ELODY: I think so. The way in which the actual conference functioned encouraged this. In the actual day-to-day practice of it, people often had to sit and listen to things in a different kind of English or language. We followed the Maori protocol for each major event of the day, which was run like a *hui*. In Maori protocol, people assemble in the big meeting house, and everybody lies or sits on mattresses waiting for their turn to speak. Each keynote address was held in that space and format. I think each keynote speaker was probably aware that he or she was standing up speaking while the audience were lying down on the floor. So there was even a physical difference in how this conference functioned as opposed to traditional conventions. In the *wharenui,* the big meeting house, you are talking to family, and when you are talking to family you can't beat around the bush. You have to live with what you have said as well.

MARY: Are you saying that the structure of the conference and its physical location lent it to becoming a conversation? As you were talking, I was thinking of the phenomenologist Gadamer, who sees conversations having a spirit of their own. You can't determine in advance where one will lead.

ELODY: Yes, the conference did have a spirit of its own. There were conventional workshops and sessions for the rest of each day. Each meeting had Maori guardians, if you like, who were watching what we were doing, even if they were not directly participating in it. They were quiet voices in a sense. There was always *karakia* or prayer and *waiata* or singing to begin each major event. Throughout the conference, people had to learn new tunes and words. So it was a kind of tangible commitment to another way of doing things. Most of the people who were there wanted to enter into it and were aware of what it was signifying and communicating. Some did find it difficult to enter in and pulled back a little. I can understand their discomfort, and I'm not meaning to be critical of them. However, what this has just made me think of is how often are we doing that to students in our classrooms. Things we do might make them uncomfortable, but do we actually give them a way out when they don't want to come with us? A lot of Maori people did a lot of bridge building and said things like, "We would like you to come along with us but you don't have to." So people had a way out. This makes me wonder if we really listen to the silent voices in our classrooms?

Living within and between Languages and Cultures

MARY: Students and teachers in New Zealand live within and between two languages and cultures. Is there a large degree of discomfort among teachers and students in New Zealand in terms of these different cultures and languages?

ELODY: Yes, I definitely think there is some discomfort, though we do acknowledge and draw in and join with aspects of Maori culture and Maori language. Our English teachers' association in New Zealand has a policy of commitment to biculturalism. That's our association, which is really a very small proportion of English teachers in general.

MARY: Not all the English teachers in New Zealand are members of the association?

ELODY: No. We have close to five hundred members. That's only about 20 percent representation.

MARY: Why is there such a low representation, and why so many silent voices?

ELODY: I think to be fair, the bicultural issue which NZATE has taken on board would be the major reason, certainly one of the divisive factors. I have been involved recently in adapting our senior English syllabus. We do have a national syllabus.

MARY: Like the National Curriculum in England?

ELODY: Yes, except our national statement is a very general one. It is not a prescriptive course but a general statement of principles and guidelines from which each school will plan its own particular course. I have been the person on contract to the Ministry of Education responsible for the rewriting of this syllabus. All through its development, that document has been headed in a clearly bicultural direction, certainly acknowledging the need for us to look at New Zealand literature, and literature in particular written by Maori authors. Of course, with that kind of commitment, you have those who immediately love it and those who do not. So we get provocative headlines in our local papers like, "New Zealand English students forced to learn Maori." Some English teachers might say things like the following, "Yes, Maori literature is important, but I don't know enough to be teaching Maori literature." However, the syllabus does not prescribe. Teachers can gradually introduce it, find their own space within it. They can make their own choice of texts to teach.

MARY: How much contact on a daily basis do Maori teachers have with English teachers?

ELODY: Well, there are very few teachers of English who are also Maori. Maori is a subject which is taught separately from English. It is growing in strength in schools through bilingual teaching, but there are still a lot of schools without a formal Maori program.

MARY: When do these Maori programs start?

ELODY: In the early grades. It's actually stronger in the early grades. Maori language teaching in early childhood is much stronger than in the upper grades. If you go up the years into secondary education, there are fewer and fewer schools able to offer bilingual programs.

MARY: What is the attitude among English teachers and New Zealanders in general toward bilingualism and biculturalism in New Zealand?

ELODY: Well again, it's really divided. You see Maori is unlike French in Canada. It isn't a language with any international status. The pragmatists would put the argument this way: What's the point? What's this language going to do for anybody? Those of us who would support it, would argue that Maori would be a language lost to the world if it were not used and encouraged in schools and throughout New Zealand. I definitely think there is a link between the death of a language and the death of a culture.

MARY: I agree. Certainly Dell Hymes's work in native languages in North America has shown this to be true. It certainly is an issue with our native and aboriginal groups here like the Cree, Mohawk, and our Inuit populations. Are there direct measures being taken to ensure that the Maori culture and language are preserved?

ELODY: Maori is recognized as an official language in New Zealand, unpopularly, but it is. There is a national languages policy that has just been adopted by the government that ensures the right of all students, if they wish, to learn Maori. I think the government is close to saying that every student in New Zealand ought to have a second language, and that's even with our current conservative government! They might not necessarily mean Maori of course. They might mean Japanese, French, or German. But it's quite an interesting principle to have put on the law books. It has put Maori in a strong position, along with the other languages as well.

MARY: What do you think will be the long-term effect of this policy on the school curriculum?

ELODY: On the one hand, we have these huge cutbacks in education, which of course always mean loss of money. Whatever language is used in second language programs will be extremely expensive. So the reality may be that it will be a slow process. On the other hand, it's there in the law books, and it's something that is being talked about. It can't be ignored.

MARY: Will that change the character of English teaching in New Zealand?

ELODY: Yes it will. It will give language a high priority, which would be wonderful. If Maori were chosen as a popular language, then it would certainly mean increasing the number of Maori teachers, which would be a revolution in itself. My sense of Maori people is that education is very important to them. They would not only be bringing the language with them, they would also be bringing a cultural perspective and ways of working that are different from white New Zealand.

MARY: What would be examples of ways of working that would be different and that might make their way into the school system?

ELODY: What strikes me is the lack of emphasis on individuality and the stress on the group and the supportiveness of that group. In terms of how most of us in English education are moving towards peer support, group work, and collaborative learning, it means that there is a tremendous amount that could be changed if we had or took on board a strong Maori influence in that direction. It would support those of us who endorse collaborative learning. So that's one particularly strong feature. The other thing, at least to me as *pakeha,* European, that Maori culture does better than our culture is listening. Respect for listening is a very strong part of the way Maori people learn and work together. When a person is speaking, the others are listening. Everyone has a right to speak in the *whanau,* the meeting house. That includes women as well. So whoever is speaking has the right to be listened to.

Speaking of Women Teachers, Authors, and Storytellers

MARY: Speaking of women, what kind of role do women play in New Zealand education? What is their influence in schools, on teaching and learning, and the lives of children?

ELODY: Similar to most other countries involved with IFTE, women dominate in terms of numbers, particularly at the elementary and secondary school levels. Most English departments are predominantly female. But as you go into the tertiary level and senior positions, you find more men. But the woman's voice is very strong. If you look at the local associations, the number of women taking initiatives is certainly very great. Our English teachers' association has a policy on gender issues.

MARY: What kind of gender issues arise for New Zealand English teachers?

ELODY: Well, sexist language is an obvious one. We are close to getting rid of sexist language, certainly at least in the groups that I work with. Another area is in the teaching of literature. We deal with the traditional texts written by men, but we look at them and engage them from different perspectives. There is encouragement and respect for the ways in which women write. New Zealand has a strong women's literary tradition, literature written by women and some New Zealand women teachers. There is Janet Frame, Katherine Mansfield, Kerry Hume, and a lot of young adult and children's literature is written by women. It is interesting to note that there is a balance between men and women writers in the Maori community.

MARY: That is interesting. Why is that so? Does that mean "the canon" then in New Zealand is different from "the canon" in North America or other countries.

ELODY: I suspect we have more women writers in New Zealand. It may be related to the *whanau*. Within the *whanau,* the women speak quite strongly. They have a tradition of using their voices. They are storytellers as men are storytellers. The only area in which women are banned in Maori culture is carving. But in terms of being teachers, authors, storytellers, and conveyors of the culture, they are very much part of it.

MARY: Do you think that in New Zealand females tell stories differently than males?

ELODY: I have an instinct to say yes there is a difference between the way men and women tell stories. I think women slip into storytelling more comfortably and less self-consciously. When men take on storytelling, maybe they do it more publicly and more consciously. I tend to think that it's more important to men that they be given an opportunity to perform.

MARY: Do you see these kinds of differences played out in classrooms in New Zealand?

ELODY: Definitely. That's where I can be absolutely quite clear about gender issues. In many classrooms, I see that boys are just so much more eager to draw attention to themselves, often through negative behavior such as noise or movement around the classroom. It's not all negative, though. Some of it is just good-natured volunteering: "Yes, we'll do that." But what I see is how the boys are up there doing, while the girls are just sitting, watching, and listening.

MARY: Well then, as a teacher educator, what do you see as the role of the teacher in situations like this?

ELODY: I do try to work with my students and raise their awareness of gender issues and help them find strategies for dealing with them. First of all, I think it comes from teachers' expectations. In my work with our student teachers, graduates from the university who come for the yearlong teacher-training course, I work with them on different strategies. For example, out of my class of twenty-four this year, I only have seven males, and after a month I drew attention to the fact that in our discussions we heard more from the six or seven male voices than the females. It takes awhile for some women to take that kind of awareness on board for themselves and do something about it at the adult level. I feel I can only make the point, and then as adults they have to take responsibility for themselves. It is important that teachers of all levels draw active attention to the behavior and attitudes which are damaging to the development of girls' self-esteem.

Choosing and Negotiating

MARY: What would that mean in terms of what English and language arts teachers would actually do in their classrooms?

ELODY: I think it means that teachers need to be very observant, watching that there is a balance between those who assume leadership, those who take initiative, and those who do not, and perhaps change group structures or even seating arrangements. You will often find in the traditional classroom a cluster of boys who like to sit together and tend to become a noise center.

MARY: Yes, but what would you see is the role of the classroom teacher if such a cluster of boys "just do prefer" to sit and work together?

ELODY: Well, my own practice in working with groups is that I like the students to choose their own people to work with. If I feel that there is a problem developing because of that choice, then I personally would have a talk with the class and say, "Look, what I'm noticing is that this group is always working together and then things happen. What do you think we should do about it. Does anybody else notice this?"

MARY: What do you do when they say they don't want to do anything about it?

ELODY: It is difficult to tamper with groups too much. It's always a delicate balancing act. I don't think I would really want to go against a "real" group preference. I'll concede this.

MARY: So you are saying that students can or should be able to negotiate roles, working styles, and the curriculum in the classroom.

ELODY: Yes, actually one of the things to do with the gender issues is that girls may need more encouragement to learn that they have negotiating power and that they can make choices. Sometimes girls and women tend to think that they haven't much to negotiate with. So it's important to get them to recognize their strengths and what they can actually do.

MARY: Do you think that most New Zealand English teachers feel they have that negotiating power?

ELODY: I really do think it's increasing. I think we've made substantial gains. Some may hold out because of a different world view, a religious-based perception of the roles of men and women.

MARY: What do you see as the role of the classroom teacher when individuals don't see things "our way"?

ELODY: Teachers need to assure students that they have a choice. My feeling is that they must be confronted at least with the issues and be free to choose knowingly and to know what the consequences of those choices are. That would be my desire. Most of our schools and even quite a few of our conservative schools deal with parental complaints quite well. The parents are invited in and are required to put their case forth, and the school puts its case forward as well. Then something is negotiated.

MARY: How does that usually work out in terms of what is negotiated?

ELODY: The most extreme version is when the parents request that a child be given a different task and withdrawn from the group. I resent it very much when the child is not given the opportunity to at least look at the issues. We do have a very conservative movement in New Zealand, and it's becoming increasingly vocal. However, I think that the tradition of whole language in New Zealand suggests that there is an acceptance within the formal structures of the importance of real reading as opposed to practice reading in basals.

MARY: What does real reading mean to you?

ELODY: Well I suppose it means being encouraged to read in such a way that you know you can pick up a book and establish your own connection with that book. It's knowing you can take a stance, a perspective, much in Louise Rosenblatt's sense of literature as exploration.

MARY: You talked earlier about the increase of Maori literature in the syllabus. How do parents and teachers react to this exploration into Maori literature?

ELODY: There is a white resistance. Some white people say Maori has nothing to do with us. But the proportion of Maori people in New Zealand is on the increase, although it is smaller than the ethnic groups of North America. But something that touches or happens in one part of the country, the rest will know about it. We've just been through a particularly significant year after 150 years of formal British contact. It was a time of celebration and also real conflict. It would be impossible to live in New Zealand now and not be touched by these issues. People have talked in New Zealand about a kind of white flight. The North Island is much more strongly populated with Maori people. There is a population drift of white conservatives.

MARY: Where do they go?

ELODY: They come to where I live, Christchurch! The whole population of Maori people in New Zealand is something like 17 percent. Christchurch has 5 percent Maori and is also the recipient of other cultures such as Vietnamese and Chinese.

MARY: How do teachers respond to these other cultures?

ELODY: They are generally well intentioned, but probably feel insecure about how to deal with students who are not English. I think that many teachers have a fear when they hear something in another language that they do not understand.

MARY: It seems to me that there is a lot of work to be done in getting teachers of English as a second language to understand Louise Rosenblatt's theory of response to literature in ESL classrooms.

ELODY: Yes, definitely. We know so little in this area. Most English second language teaching is done outside the English classroom as a separate subject. It's only in the last few years in my college that we've had specialist training groups. We have had a very traditional ESL approach here. But I also have a feeling that Maori is being taught as a second language in a very traditional way as well. The way oral Maori is taught is a reflection of the Maori culture, which is very oral. Classrooms are filled with spoken language. However, written Maori is taught in the old-fashioned grammar and formalistic approach.

MARY: I have seen a similar phenomenon in some of our native communities. I am intrigued how this formalistic, mechanistic, reductionist, institutionalized teaching of written language finds its way into these cultures. To what would you attribute this phenomenon in New Zealand?

ELODY: I think it has to do with the fact that in New Zealand the people who are least likely to succeed in education tend to be Maori students. They are badly done by the system. Many parents see their children suffering at the hands of the system and tend to think that the way in which their children are going to do well is if they can learn Standard English. That's the model for teaching, particularly for teaching writing, that has existed in New Zealand. Parents see drills and skills as a way to gain success, to pass the exams, and to get on to the tertiary system and to get into better jobs. Even those who participated with us in the conference, the Maori educators, are very insistent on English standards and the canon of classics from the British tradition. They want their children reading Shakespeare.

MARY: Is that a residual effect of the British influence in New Zealand?

ELODY: Yes. Many of these people had a classical education themselves. They do really love Shakespeare and see the reading of Shakespeare as a wonderful use of language. It's not just the British influence. There is a genuine love there as well.

MARY: Does this make it more difficult for Maori teachers to bring Maori literature into the classroom?

ELODY: No, I don't think so. There are two movements here which are side by side but complementary. Maori teachers are without exception committed to Maori culture. This is indeed a priority in their teaching. Many of them would say they see many links between stories in Maori culture and Shakespeare's stories. They see a similarity in the motifs.

MARY: It sounds like the Maori teachers are more comfortable with the two cultures and can accommodate them better than the English teachers.

ELODY: Yes, Maori people are bicultural by necessity. Most of us are monocultural.

MARY: You obviously feel very strongly about this issue of biculturalism. What in your experience has made this such a passionate topic for you?

ELODY: There's a long story there. My own experience has always been a growing one. In the late 70s I actually went back to university to do some postgraduate work, and the kinds of readings and experiences that took me into made me really examine what this business of being a New Zealander was. I would say that until then I was pretty conservative and thought of myself as a transplanted British person.

MARY: Were you born in New Zealand?

ELODY: Yes. I had a loving grandmother but she would say things like, "Oh Elody, don't speak like that, dear, you sound like a New Zealander." That was ingrained in me and I had to really shake that. As I started to explore the meaning of being a New Zealander, I found it was hard to find what that actually meant. At that same time, the Maori people were saying, "We are the people who belong here. This is our place where we stand." And I kept asking myself, "Where do I stand?" The only way I could begin to claim I belonged to New Zealand was through the Maori people and their writing, by sitting and listening and exploring the Maori language and culture. I see a lot more use of Maori literature in classrooms now than in the 70s. The Maori language is casually used. There are a lot of words that are just gradually being assumed into the language. For example, the word *whanau,* which means family. Many people would use the terms *whanau* and family interchangeably. It's not just a word, but a crucial concept. It doesn't mean mom, dad, and kids. It's a fundamental concept of Maori society, a way of communicating, valuing, and doing. There are other words like *aroha,* which means love, and *mana,* which means prestige and respect. A person's *mana* is the way in which they can stand and present themselves with some sort of dignity. A person with *mana* is highly regarded. Things like these are almost New Zealand English now, as well as originating in Maori.

MARY: I'm reminded of an article Ian Pringle wrote and titled "English as a World Language—Right Out There in the Playground: Its Many Varieties." What does this mean for English teachers, for female English teachers who you said earlier are in the majority in the elementary and secondary schools?

ELODY: I think it means that we need some strong voices to articulate what women want. We have to confront and abandon the notion of Standard English and learn to accept Englishes, varieties of Englishes. We have to get away from assessment procedures that are measurement oriented and not developmentally helpful to students' learning. We even need to put some topics aside for the moment. We have a vast amount of knowledge about teaching literature and writing. It will be self-generating. We need to break new ground. We haven't even started to dig, especially with the issues of how we can accept the many Englishes within and between different communities, contexts.

MARY: You are suggesting a strong feminist position. Would you say that most of the strong voices who have been heard to date have been largely male?

ELODY: Yes, they are certainly more published, whether it be from having more time, opportunity, friends within publishing, or a traditional sense of authority that has historically been attributed to male voices, male scholars. The written word is still very powerful, and there are just many more books and materials written by men than there are by women.

MARY: The issues are so complex.

ELODY: Yes, indeed. I remember Don McQuade's moving address at an NCTE conference. He read from a narrative piece he had written about his mother. It was a powerful address. But I kept thinking to myself: This man is doing things the way women have done things; he has told a story, slipped into story. Because he is a man, does this now mean that his male voice will give this approach authority?

Response to the Dialogues

Reading voices that have been spoken is enjoyable and seems somehow particularly appropriate for a project involving women. What is so appealing is the fluency of each interview, of the thinking process going on as each person utters. I feel very engaged by the interviews because of this fluency, because in each case the dialogue, the ideas, the topics are not finished business. I want to intervene myself in each one and ask more or make a comment. These reflections sum up the place each woman was at during the time of the interview, but leave a sense of ongoing concerns, of the never-ending fascination of learning about and through language.

Here was exemplified the spirit of inquiry. Looking back over so many years of involvement with the teaching of English, as Mary asked her to, Aviva Freedman showed her own shifts, the doubts which led to new thoughts, the questioning which still lies unanswered and continues to motivate her work.

The use of conflict and argument in the learning process as opposed to use of collaboration and consensus is complex, and one which I consider frequently as I work on developing a feminist pedagogy. Is it primarily a question of gender? I see the strengths of collaboration being in the possibility it opens up for diversity, for allowing many perspectives to be contributed. I think women enjoy considering differences and being challenged by them. We seem comfortable with accommodating. Men seem to enjoy more intellectual decisiveness, engaging in debate to win or lose the point.

These stereotypes, constructs rather than natural givens, have their limitations, which restrict both men and women. I think that the preference women show for collaboration, acceptance, and harmony should be enhanced in classrooms. But as a feminist, I am also anxious that my pedagogy leads to women changing our situations when they are hampered through oppression. I want to find ways therefore to encourage women to use "disruptive" voices, as Carol Gilligan uses the term, so that while we continue to accommodate differences, we also develop the skills and the courage to defend the right to maintain those differences.

Aviva draws from poststructuralism a concern to know more about individual voice, experience, and locations as we develop our pedagogies of writing, reading, and acting. I too struggle with these concerns. I am both excited by the challenge and disturbed by it, knowing that for all each person's reality is valid, there is also the community experience of each classroom which constantly shifts and reconstructs the individual's experiences of learning and teaching. Things change, even as we know them, becoming already in that instant the past.

Evolving, risking, listening, building, going outside and looking and starting again, learning, modeling, nurturing, reflecting, evolving—Janet Emig's conversation with Mary expounds and demonstrates all of these ingredients of teaching and learning. It also contains one other key element, energy.

For me the image which Janet conveys is that of the teacher who is always learning. Janet's moves into poetry, taking with her the experience she has from other genres which have framed her previous work, are a model of what teaching should be about. There is a risk involved because the new genre has its own traditions and expectations which, as a newcomer, Janet has to learn and to recognize what they feel like. So she doesn't just jump desperately off the cliff, flinging all her former supports away as she falls. She stays connected to her past experiences. They sustain her and also shape the particular form of poetry which will be uniquely hers.

Janet's career as she talks about it reveals many shifts, but she has kept the connections clearly from one to the next. As I watch a market-forces-driven approach encroach further on education, I see conveniently packaged, episodic learning becoming more common. What I see is in direct contrast to what Janet speaks about and models. To be attractive and competitive, schools package their curriculum into smaller, tighter, ever more discrete bundles which can be quickly assessed. They invite students to pick and choose according to their individual needs. Modularization of the curriculum is this decade's special. But I am wary of the quality of the goods. Students may be motivated by the prospect of quick success and impressed by what looks like an inviting variety. But are they encouraged to connect one learning package with another? Do they sense the nature of developmental learning skills? It seems to me they are in danger of being sold a whole lot of one-off specials.

For me, Janet's model is richer because it builds and connects progressively.

Margaret Gill develops with some fervor an idea which Janet Emig also speaks about: valuing and developing the professionalism of teachers. She is very clear that it is necessary for teachers to feel they own the intention of what they teach, the curriculum they are teaching, their methodology, and the evaluation that is practiced.

But instead of this we are seeing the very deliberate de-skilling of teachers. More often, professional decisions are being taken out of teachers' hands. The busyness of their day-to-day teaching lives is being so intensified that they have little time to reflect, plan, and develop their work. They simply function, carrying out the curriculum plan of people who are not professionally qualified in education. The recently appointed head of the National Curriculum and Assessment Development in the U.K. is the former Director of the Post Office, according to *The Guardian,* March 3, 1993. Curriculum

Development in the New Zealand Ministry of Education has been renamed Curriculum Functions. The New Right are as aware of the power of words as we are, so this name change is no accident.

I hear the frustration and concern in Margaret Gill's voice as she speaks of the stress teachers are being put under, of the difficulty of gaining time and resources for teachers to reflect on and develop their own practice, and I know we echo each other. At the very time when we have such a fund of excellent educational experience, analysis, and critique, we are being pushed by the uninformed into bad practice which, unless we resist, will influence generations.

So it is all the more important that the voices of this book and of many other educational forums keep talking, writing, exchanging theory and practice. Although for the moment the decision makers and money distributors are not listening, it must never be the case that we become silent.

How can we help learning be a safe risk for students and ourselves to take, and then become addicted to? Margaret Meek Spencer argues the need for learning to be immersed at least some of the time in play. I agree with this, because for me play means having fun; it most often, though not always, means contact with others; it means experimenting; it means practicing, playing at what I have seen adults doing in the real world. It is a kind of rehearsing, but because it is engaged in a complete framework of fantasy, it takes on the validity of "real" experience. My own memories of playing as a child are memories of "how things were." I recall my play as if it were real. Indeed it was a crucial part of how I learned my way in life.

In connection with issues to do with women and girls in education, play is a very important factor. Play is an extremely powerful influence in socializing boys and girls into their expected, gendered codes of behavior. Girls play with dolls, play mothers, nurses, and secretaries. Their play activities are usually less aggressive, less mobile, less active than the play of boys. Very much approved of as part of girls' play are the activities of reading, writing, and even of "playing school." For boys, heavier toys and tools, physical action, sport, and war games are typical activities. Play is a very important way of learning and has much for us to apply in the classroom, but not without questioning some of the ways in which unthinkingly it constructs oppressive models for girls' and boys' learning.

The National Curriculum as it has developed in the U.K. since Henrietta Dombey's discussion with Mary has fulfilled both her positive hopes and her worst fears. Certainly at the beginning, the general direction of the

English statement produced some positive ideas about language teaching, and the initial tests at Key Stage One took a form which, although very time consuming, did improve the practice of many teachers.

However, since then there has been much to concern teachers. The publication of the results of tests in league table format, the major change in the nature of the tests, increasing restriction on classroom teaching styles, a very prescriptive English syllabus, and confusion about the tests for the higher key stages, all unite many English teachers in opposition to the changes.

I am very aware how vigilant we have to be at every stage of party political interference in education. Yet at the very time our energies are being called upon to engage in such vigilance, the restructuring of education continues at a pace which leaves teachers without time for the necessary reflection and development of strategies for opposition.

As top-down power operations become the way governments bring about their will, I am afraid of how we all become reaccustomed to such ways of working. It is not just the restrictions put on the syllabus statements, not just the testing and reporting procedures that I find objectionable, but the whole ethos which prepares people to accept their place, to do what they are told, to try to please for fear of the power of the person in authority being turned against them.

I know in every respect it will be women and girls who suffer most in such a climate. Though we have worked hard for equity, for acceptance of a more assertive role for girls and women, we are still at the vulnerable frontier stage of establishing these gains. Assaults on the concept of empowering women and girls have a high chance of success. Since I have been here in the U.K., there have been some interesting responses to the improving academic achievement of girls by contrast with boys, especially in language and mathematics. Calls for a change to the testing, a change in content, changes in the style of teaching, going back to more competitive streaming and less group work have been the response. If competitiveness and pugnaciousness become again the basic principles of curriculum and the modes of teaching practice, we will, like Virginia Woolf in *Three Guineas,* need to challenge them and employ tactics to disrupt their reinstatement.

To work in the Caribbean as a teacher of English in a time of emerging national interest in the indigenous culture is obviously full of challenge and probably a good deal of struggle. In New Zealand similar developments are taking place, both for Maori voices and for *pakeha* (white) voices, both needing to free themselves from colonization. Patricia Symmonds's talk of so many new writers and the discovery of some temporarily "lost" works makes me hope that many of them will gain international readers as well as Caribbean.

I find Patricia's comments on the recommendation by the Status of Women Commission for education to go coeducational very interesting. I wonder if they are still satisfied with that choice? There is controversy over the success of coeducation for girls, and it is a complex issue in our subject particularly. Although they achieve good results in English, women have not gone on to gain higher positions in educational administration or in the tertiary institutions. To play devil's advocate, is there a connection between this failure and the fact that, in my experience as well as Patricia's, girls frequently end up reading texts which have been selected to keep the boys interested? Of course the other very substantial area of their reading is the romance genre, another resource which makes sure they are socialized to know how to behave, usually as competitors with each other for the favors of men.

There are still so many very basic issues to address!

Selected Bibliography for Elody Rathgen

Language and Schooling (co-authored with F. Johnson). 1985. In *Language, Schooling, and Society,* edited by S. N. Tchudi, 145–150. Upper Montclair, N.J.: Boynton/ Cook.

Is High School English Gender Based? 1986. *International Digest.*

Writing and Learning: A Look at the New South Wales and New Zealand Curriculum Statements on the Teaching of Writing. 1988. In *Teaching Writing, K–12,* edited by R. D. Walshe and P. Marsh, 80–92. Melbourne: Dellasta Pty. Ltd.

The Word Process (co-authored with A. Carruthers, D. Philips, and P. Scanlan). 1991. New Zealand: Longman Paul.

Say It with Words: A Text for 6th and 7th Form English (co-authored with P. Scanlan). 1991. New Zealand: Caxton Educational.

New Zealand Literature Guidelines: The Bone People (co-authored with R. Davey). 1993. New Zealand: Longman Paul.

Feminism and Postmodernism in the English Classroom: What's the Difference? 1993. *English International* (International Assembly of NCTE), *1(1),* 15–26.

Poetryworks: User-friendly Resources. 1994. Christchurch, New Zealand.

Patricia Symmonds

P atricia Symmonds and I never engaged in a face-to-face conversation. I remember our first telephone conversation in July 1991. She phoned me in response to my letter inviting her to become a part of the international dialogue. That same summer, thanks to technology, our conversation brought us closer together, she in Barbados and I in Montreal. I now have a better appreciation of what it means to work in the Caribbean as a teacher of English in a time of emerging national interest in the indigenous culture. It is full of challenge and a good deal of struggle that includes "lost works" of significant Caribbean voices. It includes controversy about the success of coeducation for girls and Standard English.

The Challenge of English Teaching in Barbados and the Caribbean

Talking about Standards and Teaching as a Female Profession

MARY:　When we spoke last week, you expressed an interest in two issues: the issue of Standard English and the issue of teaching as a female profession.

PATRICIA:　Yes. I see these issues in relation to language, but they include literature as well. I think they are indivisible. Currently we are experiencing some problems in Barbados and in the Caribbean. The first relates to the issue of Standard English. Some people of influence downplay its importance. I think it is a complex issue. In some of the articles I have written, such as in *On Language and Life-Styles,* I talked about how in the previous years Barbadians aimed at mastering Standard English as a means of self-improvement and social mobility. I would like to quote from one of these articles: "The post-independence era, however, and the teaching of West Indian History, have helped to make people aware of what may be called their Barbadian identity. Unfortunately this awareness has created some confusion in an age where there is already too much confusion. Language has always been a part of identity, but what many people do not appear to understand is that language also has global implications."

MARY:　What implications do you see for language and learning today?

PATRICIA:　The message then was that one should master Standard English. Today the message is a confused one. People are encouraged to use their own dialect and to recognize that Creole in the Caribbean is their language. Yet the pressure to master Standard English is still a societal concern. Prior to the 60s, the Bible had an enormous effect on Barbadians' learning and use of language. You could see this in their use of particular turns of phrase and idioms of the Bible.

　　It is interesting to note as well that the role of women is very evident in teaching in Barbados. The majority of teachers tend to be women. In fact, over 60 percent are women. The gap has been narrowing somewhat, but there is a lack of male teachers in the school system. You can think of teaching as a female profession with a female register. If you believe that there is a register of language that is particularly female, it would influence the way in which children write.

MARY: Is this proportion of female to male teachers the norm at the elementary or secondary level?

PATRICIA: Both.

MARY: Why is there a lack of male presence in the schools in Barbados?

PATRICIA: Unfortunately, because of the changes in society, boys tend not to view teaching as a worthwhile career. Thus there are not enough male role models. The issue is complicated by the fact that the role of the teacher has become more complex. Teachers are expected to be social workers, psychologists, mothers, fathers, counselors, instructors. Before 1961, when free education was introduced in Barbados, we had a narrower ability range. Now we are dealing with a population of 20,000 in secondary schools, as opposed to years ago when we had a population of 2,000. We have more social problems now than before. We no longer have the extended family. There is an absence of docility, respect for authority has diminished, and there are more disciplinary problems in the schools. Teachers say they have to work very hard motivating students.

Another influence on language use and our curriculum is the changes which are occurring in North America and the world. Because of the proliferation of books and technology and easier communication, our curriculum has changed and our language is changing. Many of our structures are still within the British tradition, but spelling, vocabulary, and pronunciation, for example, are being affected by North American influence.

Teachers have to adapt to many new trends, including coeducation. You must remember that coeducation, which has been in North America for some time, is relatively new here and was only introduced into our schools in 1979. There have been some problems as a consequence of this, especially in the secondary schools, which have expanded in numbers.

MARY: How many secondary schools do you have in Barbados?

PATRICIA: We have twenty-two and another one is being built.

MARY: How do the teachers feel about coeducation and their students' literacy? You referred earlier to a female register of language use.

Reading the Tastes of Boys and Girls

PATRICIA: Well, among some teachers of English here, there is the perception that boys do not have the ability to use language as well as girls. Some feel that the girls read more and mature earlier and that boys, especially in the lower schools, are more interested in activities that require motor skills. These perceived and recognized differences between boys and girls in our schools present new problems for teachers. For instance, in the selection of literature texts, teachers of English now have to devise methods and choose texts more carefully that will appeal to both genders. I think more dialogue with schools in North America, where coeducation has been a fact and has had more of a historical tradition, could help us.

MARY: What kinds of books do boys and girls like to read in Barbados?

PATRICIA: We have found that in the second form, which would be your grade 7, girls will read *boys'* books, but boys do not read *girls'* books. For example, girls will read *Tom Sawyer, Treasure Island,* and Caribbean literature like *Hurricane.* For some reason, *Moby Dick* is not popular with the girls. This problem of choosing texts carefully is something teachers experience daily, especially in the third form. Of course I realize there is always a danger in generalizing. Some teachers have reported that they have no problems. However, for others it is a real problem. Some say that traditional girls' books like *Jane Eyre* and *Pride and Prejudice* don't appeal to the boys, although the character of Rochester does seem to appeal to the boys. It is interesting to note that the tales from Shakespeare generally appeal to both girls and boys. I think this has something to do with his universality.

MARY: That's interesting. I recall when talking to Elody Rathgen about Maori educators in New Zealand, she commented on how Maori educators and parents want their children reading Shakespeare. She says it's not just a residual effect of the British influence in New Zealand, but there is a genuine love there as well. So you are saying that there are a number of reasons why teachers in Barbados believe they should and want to continue to teach Shakespeare.

PATRICIA: Yes, definitely.

MARY: What about pressure to include popular and national culture in the classroom? Do teachers in Barbados feel pressure to do that?

PATRICIA: Only up to a certain point. With the upsurge of nationalism and the movement towards Caribbean unity, we see this especially in art, drama, and music. We have changed from the Cambridge examination body and since 1979 have the Caribbean Examination Council. That influences the books students are asked to read. I should like to come back to the point of choosing books carefully and choosing ones that have appeal to both genders. It is interesting that the *Chrysalids, To Kill a Mockingbird,* and *Great Expectations* do not seem to present a problem of gender difference. They seem to appeal to both boys and girls.

MARY: Why do you think that they have this appeal to both genders?

PATRICIA: I think it is because the themes are universal. They speak to the human condition. They have strong male characters in them. There is action in them. I am not fond of Dickens myself, but his books do appeal to the boys as well as the girls.

MARY: Speaking of taste and texts that appeal to students, how do they feel about poetry?

PATRICIA: Well, now that we have come to poetry, I can see that there is more of a problem here. Perhaps it has something to do with the fact that we live in an age of prose rather than poetry. Some teachers report difficulties in teaching poetry. In the second form, there appears to be no problem. However, it's in grades 10, 11, and 12 that it becomes a problem. Perhaps this may be because boys at that age are self-conscious of their roles as males, or they are less sensitive and don't like reflective poetry or don't like to engage in abstraction. Whatever the reasons, there are then *good reasons* to have a variety of types of poems accessible to students. Boys tend to respond better to poems of action. We have a delightful anthology here called *Talk of the Tamarinds.*

MARY: That's an interesting title. What does "tamarinds" mean?

PATRICIA: It refers to a tree with an acid fruit that children love. It is made into tamarind candy balls, which again the children love. There are a number of very good poems in this anthology which appeal to the children and they are not only West Indian poems. Some of my colleagues maintain that response to poetry depends on the ability or interest of the students. On the other hand, as a judge in some school literary competitions, I have found poems written by boys which were of a high quality. There are certain poems that the girls respond to and that the boys find mushy, such as the poem "How Do I Love Thee," by Elizabeth Barrett Browning, or "Dover Beach," by Matthew Arnold. Girls seem to like the Yeats poem "Aedh Wishes for the Cloths of Heaven" with those lovely striking lines: "I have spread my dreams under your feet / Tread softly because you tread on my dreams." But boys are not comfortable with these poems. In a sixth form or perhaps a fifth if they have a certain reaction initially, their intellect is so developed that they can appreciate the quality of the poem.

MARY: Are you saying then that the girls in Barbados tend to be more responsive to poetry than the boys?

PATRICIA: Yes. There are some boys who do not relate to poetry at any level. Some boys think poetry is something feminine. Therefore, teachers have to choose poems carefully and even short stories. Some teachers say that there are students in the secondary school who appear unable to write an original short story. Before, the students were asked to write an essay and a short story. Now, the examination demands a short story. It will be interesting to see whether exposure to and the study of that form will make a difference to the output. Some teachers say the short story is a difficult genre for some students to write in and that it requires particular talents such as imagination and an understanding of human behavior.

MARY: Wouldn't that depend on the previous opportunities for pleasurable experiences with stories the students have had? I think that children derive any written language system or literary tradition from what they experience of it.

PATRICIA: Yes. This relates to something I mentioned earlier about the loss of the extended family. One result is that parents don't have time to read to their children as they used to. We really don't have much of that anymore. As well, there are many counterattractions to books such as videos, television, and other new forms of technology and new stresses being put on families and working parents that were not there years ago. In school, teachers feel there is so much reading to be done, there is not as much time for enjoyment of stories and poems. I remember vividly how my mother used to read poems to me and how much I enjoyed them.

MARY: So teachers feel pressured to cover a canon of prescribed English texts which students must read.

PATRICIA: Yes, to the extent that they are expected to cover a wide syllabus in two years. In the Barbados Association of English Teachers, we felt that students were required to read too many texts. It is significant that John Wickham, editor of *Bim Magazine* and himself a writer of creative stories, has observed that the standard of creative writing in the Caribbean has dropped from its peak in the late 1940s and early 1950s, although there have always been a number of Caribbean authors like Timothy Callender, Sir Vidia Naipaul, and Samuel Selvow who have produced work of outstanding worth. And whatever poetry is being composed is by women in Jamaica and it is stimulated by anger.

MARY: What do you feel has provoked these angry voices?

PATRICIA: Part of it has to do with our social history because much of our writing takes the form of social commentary. I don't want to pontificate here because I haven't given that much thought to it.

MARY: Are these angry voices which are given expression in poetry just coming from Jamaica or other parts of the Caribbean?

PATRICIA: Well that's interesting. We here in Barbados do not have many women writers. There are a few like Elizabeth Clarke, Linda Walroad, and Esther Philips, one of my students. Esther Philips wrote an excellent book of poems in 1983. It is part of the Poetry Chapbook Series, University of the West Indies. There are a number of other fine Caribbean poets. Ameryl Johnson has written an anthology, *The Long Road to Nowhere.* She is from Trinidad but lives in England. Elizabeth Clarke wrote *Mother Africa* in 1972. Merle Collins wrote *Because the Dawn Breaks.* There is Valerie Bloom, who is Jamaican and wrote *Touch Me Tell Me,* and of course there is Louise Bennett, who has written in dialect.

There are other Jamaicans such as Jean Goulbourne, Lorna Goodison, Pamela Mordecai, Rachel Manley, and Barbara Ferland. Some of their poems deal with nature, love relationships, and the experiences of people who use Creole as their main language. Yvonne Weeks is from Montserrat and has recently published a book, *Deep in the Blueness of Me.* Her poems are of passion, social commentary, and she has written one about her grandmother.

MARY: Would these writers' texts find their way into the classrooms in Barbados?

PATRICIA: Yes, there is the tendency to include Caribbean literature in the curriculum. We also have a few short story writers such as Anna Jones. She is a teacher and a principal of one of our private schools. Millicent Fyfe and Monica Skeete are also considered writers of merit. In Jamaica, Hazel

Campbell has written a number of short stories, and Olive Senior's *Summer Lightning and Other Stories* is a vivid, imaginative work. I have discovered that my own mother wrote a few short stories in the 30s. Reflecting on her work, I must acknowledge that she was certainly ahead of her time. She wrote one story about a girl who committed suicide because she discovered she was pregnant. Certainly this was not something to be written about or talked about then. John Wickham has uncovered this story. I want to read and assess it more critically.

MARY: Do you write stories or poems yourself?

Changing the Balance

PATRICIA: I wrote one or two plays and one or two poems when I was at school. After I began teaching, I spent time producing plays. However, I have written two poem in recent times, one of which was published before the "Introduction" to the *Report of the National Commission on the Status of Women.*

I was at the time deputy chair of the Status of Women. I had also served as chair of the National Advisory Committee on Women's Affairs. In those days there was a tremendous amount of discrimination against women. We recommended that schools become coeducational. There are reasons now why there are so few short stories. In the 1940s, this was a time for struggle and the people's awareness of inequities and social justice. All the rage went into creative work. Now, I think people are more complacent. Because of free education, all that type of talent is now in universities.

Ian Macdonald is a poet, novelist, and journalist from Trinidad who went to Cambridge. He lives in Guyana and has done a great deal of writing on a variety of subjects. John Wickham says that practicing and prestigious writers like Ian Macdonald and Mervyn Morris have suggested that young writers who would formerly have produced their own works are now attending university and "writing about writing." Instead of being creative, they are being critical and writing criticism. Before, we had individuals who were producing stories and poems, but they were not in the universities. Now, these types of individuals go to the University of the West Indies and their energies are channeled into academic theses.

MARY: Do you think the shift you describe represents a loss for the Barbados and Caribbean literary tradition?

PATRICIA: We still have a body of literature, however, and famous writers like Derek Walcott and Edward Kamau Braithwaite. Edward Braithwaite is Barbados's best known and most famous poet, and he has gained international recognition. A former student of Harrison College, a Barbados scholar, and graduate of Cambridge University, he lectures in history at the Mona Campus of the University of the West Indies. His main anthology, *The Assistant,* is used at both secondary and tertiary levels. One of his most popular poems, "The Dust," is often dramatized and recited at national festivals and school presentations throughout the Caribbean. *Odale's Choice,* his major drama, and an Africanized version of *Antigone* are also studied in schools and widely performed by drama groups.

Research isn't a total loss. It's just a pity we can't have both. But I think that that's beginning to happen again. Things I think will eventually sort themselves out. There were no female equivalents in the 50s. Women were not emancipated and women's interests were stifled. Now we are beginning to see a change. I hope we have changed and are changing the balance. I hope that we will see more women writers.

MARY: Is there anything else you would like to bring up or talk about?

PATRICIA: Yes, before we finish, I would like to bring up two things. First, we have had a recent development project which was funded by University of the West Indies-U.S. aid and included the development of curriculum. It is called the Primary Education Project. The program is to provide learning experiences for children whose first language is not Standard English. It is interesting that all the teachers who worked on this project are women. They have selected English grammatical structures or patterns not generally found in the children's home language and used them as the focal point of the unit. Children are encouraged to talk freely, but are motivated to use the Standard English structures which they have been taught.

MARY: What is your own position on Standard English?

PATRICIA: One cannot ignore an international language. It is a commonplace that countries use internationally accepted English in trade and in political, social, and diplomatic negotiations. To limit oneself to a local dialect is to ostracize oneself from the mainstream of activity at a time when all countries recognize their interdependence. Further, a local dialect is understood only in the environment in which it is used. But the Caribbean islands on the whole, and Barbados in particular, rely on immigration and tourism for economic stability. The major English-speaking countries all have dialects—the United States, Australia, Canada, New Zealand, and England, which has twenty-five. But Standard English is their official language. Standard English is also the lingua franca of the Caribbean. There would be linguistic chaos if each island employed its own dialect. We owe it to our children to encourage the highest standards of correct Standard English.

MARY: Is teaching an appreciation of Caribbean literature and use of Creole a priority in Barbados for English teachers?

PATRICIA: In the Caribbean, generally the medium of instruction is Standard English, and children's work must be in Standard English across the curriculum. But in oral presentations and in written dialogue children are allowed to use Creole in situations where nonstandard expression would be expected. I mention the Primary Education Project as it relates to what I said at the beginning about Standard English.

The second point concerns a 1987 functional competencies survey. I was chair of the advisory committee, and on the whole we found that females performed better than males on such items as responding to government information, family planning, respecting the rights of others. The males did better on computer-related and technical items.

MARY: You have spoken a lot about gender differences and from a number of perspectives. One of the issues we are facing in our Canadian educational system, and I think other countries as well are facing the same issue, is the increased multicultural character of our schools. Is this an issue in Barbados?

PATRICIA: Yes, it is. We have had a great amount of immigration from other Caribbean territories. Before, our population was black (Afro-European) and white. We are quickly becoming more cosmopolitan. This has had implications for schooling in Barbados, as, for example, in our dress codes and attitudes towards religious freedom. We are managing to integrate and have had to adapt and become more tolerant. Politically, we have always had a pretty stable government. It was only in 1937 we had a riot. Basically the relationships between blacks and whites have been distant but quite harmonious. There has not been as much social mixing as there might have been or could be. We have a black governor general, black prime minister, black members of Parliament in the Lower House, and both blacks and whites in the Senate. Some people are clamoring for economic empowerment and feel much of the wealth of Barbados is owned by whites.

MARY: How is the relationship between blacks and whites reflected in your schools?

PATRICIA: I wouldn't want to generalize about that. It would differ from individual to individual and school to school. Children are still selected by choice and ability. There are more white children in our schools. We still have a common entrance examination. On the whole, the relationships between the races are good. Out of school there is not as much social integration as we would like, although this is changing. I see it as less a problem of race and more a problem of gender. You can go right back to the days when teaching and nursing were the only professions for women to think about entering. Now, I think it's a question of qualifications. When we appoint teachers, we appoint Caribbean people as well as individuals from other countries. Naturally, if you are looking at providing jobs, you will offer them to your own first, providing they have the qualifications. I see it as a gender issue more than a race issue.

MARY: So it's understandable then, as you said earlier, that teaching looks like a female profession in Barbados.

PATRICIA: Yes indeed.

Reflections

The comments made during the interview reflect Aviva Freedman's interest in "the way in which gender manifests itself in writing," but also some reservation as to whether "some of the models that are presented are in fact as gender specific as people claim, as opposed to stances or styles." She was of the view that previous conferences had tended to play down and "gloss over differences," and she sensed a reluctance to confront issues. She perceived "resistance among researchers at the '78 and '86 conferences to engage in any kind of oppositional discourse" and deemed this something of a defect.

Aviva recognized that each school of thought would have its own perspective and that even within any one school each individual would have his or her own perspective and there was need to recognize and accept these realities. The question was, then, just how could students be helped to improve their writing skills and competencies. Should they be helped to write for different disciplines, for example biology or law? In any case, the vital question would be how best to broaden the role and learning outcomes of specific tasks.

All these questions needed to be considered in the context of the recognition that different people were likely to have preferences for, say, the "abstract" or the "concrete" and that the teacher was then faced with the question of how to "respond to such diversity." One approach seemed to be that of helping teachers to recognize and be sensitive to the range of learning styles noted in the research literature and especially to be aware of their own preferences.

The kind of approach which Aviva perceived as being more typical of women in general was illustrated by the following example: It would be okay to say that was a stupid idea. But it would not be okay to say that about somebody's personality and personhood. In other words, a non-confrontational approach would be preferred to an oppositional one. She also looked briefly at the "really grass-roots supports" needed by teachers, not only through parents but nonprofessionals in the community. Finally, the view was put forward that some of the preferences and tendencies perceived might well be "entirely a question of socialization . . . as well as individual stylistic preferences."

Margaret Gill was concerned with, among other things, means of empowering both teachers and learners, with finding "a way of working with our children in the classrooms that maximizes their sense of what they can do in their own world and in their own learning." Fundamental to all such considerations was the kind of relationship existing between teacher and learner, and the extension of this relationship to include remedial help from parents and other community persons who could come in and work alongside the classroom teacher.

Basically, then, this approach required acceptance of the learner as an individual capable of being self-directed even in the childhood stage, as well as diminishing dependence on others. Such increasing independence was also needed by the teacher in his or her professional role. Consequently, there was need to see the teacher in a different perspective, not just as a passive tool of the researcher, but as having "a role in generating and clarifying and making more relevant the researcher's question." And tough questions have to be asked, such as "How to improve classrooms?"

To answer this, it would be essential to help teachers identify the good things they do and to determine, as far as possible, "the best kind of support to help teachers identify the good things they are already doing." Similarly, important concerns relate to who are the most suitable resource persons for involvement in the classroom context, improving interaction among teachers, encouraging risk taking among teachers, and the like.

Solutions to some of these may well require empowering teachers. Thus "the prescriptions of textbooks move outside the control of the teachers, and that takes away part of the teachers' ownership of their classrooms." Likewise, undue emphasis on testing may also be inimical to the risk taking deemed desirable since "the pressure of forces weighing on teachers makes them feel they have either been a success or failure, depending on the scores the kids get in these tests."

A further comment related to the recognition of the value of small-group learning, which tended to change the entire climate of the classroom and generally led to a "redistribution" of power, in which students shared directly. However, it was to be noted that the kind of teacher empowerment envisaged would often appear threatening to administrators, unless it was possible to involve these very persons directly in the relevant decision making about the kind of procedures desired and needed to attain specified objectives.

Henrietta Dombey's most urgent concern was about the proposal for a National Curriculum. She saw this development as having potential for good, but also as being possibly inimical to the best interests of education. Indeed, to date "we can't say with good conscience [it] is like the best practice that we have seen." Some approaches to language itself seem defective. In truth, "Certainly questionable is the idea that language is learned in a strictly linear fashion with a preordained route that every child will follow so that any child can be assessed in terms of how far he or she is along that route."

A basic concern for Henrietta was therefore "an evaluation system . . . to reflect children's ability to read in a way that relates what they read to their own experience." Undue emphasis on assessment may indeed lead a teacher to "teach new lessons in old ways and thereby experience only dissatisfaction and anxiety and pass on much of that to the children in his or her charge." Thus she advocated greater freedom for the teacher: "if schools could give teachers more opportunity, with some assistance from the outside world . . . to explore their own strengths," there would be considerable benefit for all concerned, teacher, student, and school alike.

Tied in with the whole curriculum and assessment changes projected is the importance of adequate support for the teacher, especially with respect to preservice and inservice provisions. And just as critical is the need for and importance of facilitating teacher interaction across all levels. Hence, "[W]e need to make teacher training more of a collaborative enterprise between the institutions of higher education and the schools themselves ... bringing teachers into teacher education institutions and having the professors go into the schools and teach."

Finally, the importance of the school-home relationship should not be forgotten or overlooked, and there is need "to invite parents into school in a different spirit ... we have to invite parents in to contribute ... to share something of their own expertise." Logically, as well, there is need to pay closer attention to the family itself for "the enabling family seems to be essentially a democratic family where children's voices count, where what they say is taken notice of not just in terms of all the niceties, but in terms of substance."

In conclusion, Henrietta supported the contention that teachers and students alike needed to be empowered. Teachers "need to see that children are not powerless individuals waiting to be energized by being given the information and the skills by a teacher." Hence the need for vision and willingness to change: "When it comes to teaching and learning and curriculum change, we shouldn't sit too comfortably with our assumptions."

Janet Emig is strongly supportive of the more liberalized approach to what is considered "acceptable" in research and in professional writing: "There is now a more generous definition of what inquiry is or can be." The new approach has significance for the classroom teacher, now allowing people, including women, "to trust and believe in our own experiences." There are other spinoffs as well, for example, moving towards the acceptability of using the first person. As a consequence there may be a different approach to writing theses and so forth.

Attention was also devoted to matters such as the limited membership in professional organizations and noticeable tendencies to undesirable separation of roles, for example "to separate the curriculum developers from the evaluators." This is deemed undesirable, for when teachers fill both roles, they "can begin to make connections between the assessment that they themselves have done, based on what they know, and the research."

Like Henrietta, Janet saw the need for closer relationships between "university people who are sometimes perceived as the theorists and the researchers, and classroom teachers who tend to see themselves as being the practitioners." But even more is needed. Structures need to be developed which will accord to parents a far more significant role than they now have and which will in fact facilitate multiple interaction among teachers, parents, administrators, and students themselves. What is needed is "empowerment" of those now with relatively little power. As Janet puts it, "I see teachers organizing themselves so that as professionals they are in charge of curriculum and teaching." Logically, also, there is need to make much more effective use of available technology, for example for teleconferencing, so as to facilitate interaction among teachers in widely separated areas.

Janet also showed some concern about how children could best be helped to "learn to write" not just the words, but to acquire an interest in expressing their own ideas, bearing in mind that children differ from each other. She therefore supported more involvement of youngsters in open discussion in the classroom and greater expression of their own ideas, that is, to "allow these [ideas] legitimacy inside the classroom." Finally, the teachers must be prepared to recognize the "legitimacy of many ways of knowing and risk venturing forth into alternate ways of setting forth what we're learning."

Margaret Meek Spencer was critical of the undesirable separation of reading from "other forms of language, its uses and functions." She argued that "once we begin to think of reading and writing in social contexts, then our view of teaching, learning, and literacy is bound to change." Moreover, this inevitable change is bound to be affected and influenced by changes in computer-related technology with respect to both reading and writing.

She also argued for giving greater freedom to the teacher, especially from "the need to produce test scores," and she was firm in the belief that teachers would be greatly helped by recognizing that "there is nothing different about learning to read than learning other things." Like other interviewees, Margaret also argued for more and better interaction among teachers at different levels, and she would wish to see primary teachers functioning in secondary schools and vice versa.

Particular attention was paid to Vygotsky and his work, especially in relation to the notion of language as a tool. Emphasizing the importance of play as a learning mechanism, Margaret argued that "play is really serious business" and "every bit as serious as . . . learning to stack bricks up."

A particular criticism was that often the school exerted an inhibiting effect on the child's learning: "It narrows down a lot that would have remained as potential [in children] if we hadn't used the authority of school to school it." One more approach would therefore be to use the school context more effectively as a social one, "as a social institution."

The kind of approach advocated would pay much more attention to cultural influences and would thus attach much more importance to autobiographical items as sources of information and influence. And this approach might well lessen some of the difficulties stemming from different perceptions of teachers and pupils from different social classes.

Related to this perspective is the need to pay greater attention to the importance of the home-school relationship. As Margaret put it, "Children are [often] inhibited not because they can't do it, not because they're afraid of the teacher, but because they're looking all the time to find out what the discourse rules are."

Specifically, Margaret Meek Spencer argues for a very different approach to the teaching of reading. Her perspective is especially well expressed in the following comments:

> [I]f you want to read a modern novel, you don't first have to take a course on how to read older literature . . . . You assume that the mastery you have already can be stretched to something which you have never encountered before. . . . [W]hat always worries me is that people who don't write teach writing, and people who don't read teach reading. It does seem a bit loony if you were to invite a non-piano player teacher to teach your child to play the piano.

So, in the potentially productive exercise of teaching reading, we should use a different approach and should seek "to find out ways in which teachers can collaborate with their students so that being a student is not a subsidiary role; it's a learning and teaching role. It's a partnership."

Selected Bibliography
for Patricia Symmonds

On Language and Life Styles. 1989. Bridgetown, Barbados.

Louise M. Rosenblatt

I remember my first conversation with Louise Rosenblatt. It was in 1978 when she was a keynote speaker at the Quebec Secondary English Teachers' annual conference at the Mount Royal Hotel in Montreal. I attended her session on response to literature, and I remember my feeling of respect and admiration for her clarity of mind and sensitivity to readers. I had just read Literature as Exploration, *a book that changed my teaching, significantly influenced my own doctoral dissertation on* Middle Grade French Immersion Children's Perceptions and Productions of English and French Narrative Discourse, *and continues to influence and inform my research. What I remember most vividly and with appreciation was her openness and enthusiasm when I phoned her to request our conversation for this book.*

I originally had asked her to write an epilogue that would summarize the interviews. Louise was emphatic in her response:"I don't want to write an epilogue and put closure or summary to these individuals' thoughts. I consider myself part of the conversation of English teachers."Whether she knew it at the time or not, she had a clearer vision of what this book is about than I did. My original prospectus included an introductory chapter that would contextualize the interviews within a Bakhtinian theoretical framework. Thanks to Louise and an anonymous reviewer, as mentioned in the prologue, I abandoned that idea.

This conversation with Louise took place via telecommunications in December 1991. She was at her home in Princeton, and I was in my office at McGill. She was just about to leave for a trip to Puerto Rico. It was a cold, snowy day in Montreal, but I could sense Louise's warmth and empathy. She may not have wanted to write an epilogue for this book, but in appreciation for her contribution to English teachers for the last fifty years, she does get to have the last word in this international dialogue, which she extends with her metaphor of communities and classrooms harmonizing together.

Looking Back and Looking Forward

MARY: In our discussions about setting up this conversation via telecommunications, multiculturalism and cultural pluralism have been some recurrent themes that have emerged. Maybe we can open up our conversation today there.

LOUISE: Yes, recognition and respect for all the strands that make up our society has been a theme of mine for years. Multiculturalism is much discussed, and you might even say propagandized, at present in the United States. As I was reading the paper this morning, I thought of all the other places in the world where multicultural situations have created terrible problems. I was thinking of places like Yugoslavia and perhaps the USSR. I have been very concerned about the forms that the push for multiculturalism has sometimes taken in the United States.

I'm looking at things from, I am afraid, a long perspective. I look back to 1946, almost half a century ago. At the end of World War II, I was a member of a committee of the National Council of Teachers of English, called the Intergroup Relations Committee, headed by Marion Edman, a very dedicated worker in that field and in the field of elementary education. We talked about intergroup relations and cultural pluralism then. We now talk about multiculturalism. As a member of that committee, I was very much concerned with the same kinds of problems we now see in schools. The change in terminology has many subtle implications. In June 1946, I published an article on the subject in *College English* and I edited for the committee a special issue of the *English Journal* dedicated to the theme that the teaching of language and literature can be a means of nourishing the democratic appreciation of each person as a human being regardless of racial, religious, national, or social labels. I'm proud that I was able to get people like Thomas Mann, James Farrell, Ruth Benedict, Horace Kallen, and leaders in other fields as well as English to write articles for that issue.

MARY: You were actually a student of Ruth Benedict's at one time.

LOUISE: Yes. I was a student of hers first when she was an assistant to Franz Boas. As an undergraduate at Barnard College, Columbia University, I took work in anthropology with Franz Boas. My major was English, but my interest in anthropology led to the compromise of taking a doctorate in comparative literature at the University of Paris. On my return, while I was teaching at Barnard College, I did two years of graduate work in anthropology with Franz Boas and Ruth Benedict.

MARY: How have those experiences and individuals influenced and shaped your ideas on cultural pluralism, context, and text?

LOUISE: They had a very profound influence because I learned very early to respect other cultures and to realize that there were many different ways that human beings organize or structure their basic human needs and capacities. The anthropological study of other cultures counteracts the tendency to reject the different and to assume that ours is in all respects superior. In those days, following the war against Nazi racism and fascism, the emphasis particularly was on combating racism and belief in the inferiority or superiority of any particular race. Indeed the whole concept of "race" was questioned scientifically—as it continues to be. Despite present-day discrimination, it is hard for young people today to understand how much racism impregnated our society even as we were fighting it abroad.

The reason I keep coming back to 1946 is that I see certain changes that have come about and hence the need to see what our future attitudes should be. In 1946, for instance, in that issue of the *English Journal,* we used the expression "cultural pluralism" which had been coined by Horace Kallen, professor of philosophy at the New School for Social Research, and Alain Locke, an African American as we would say today, who taught philosophy at Howard, Harvard, and other universities. Recall that this was before the Supreme Court decision making segregated schools unconstitutional, and before the civil rights movement of the 60s. They were the first to use the term cultural pluralism, by which they meant the recognition of the dignity and value of all the cultures that came together in the United States. At that time, they were reacting against the melting pot idea—the notion that somehow everybody had to be assimilated to the WASP, white Anglo-Saxon Protestant, middle-class image. The important thing about cultural pluralism is that, while we were emphasizing the importance and the dignity of each group and of each individual in the group, we were also emphasizing the importance of unity. In other words, there was diversity within unity, as Horace Kallen expressed it.

In 1978, I was writing about the same problems in an essay on Walt Whitman and "the new ethnicity" published in the *Yale Review.* The term *ethnicity* had recently appeared as a new term in the dictionary, reflecting the fact that one aspect of cultural pluralism—its recognition of pride in one's "roots"—had gained momentum. We have come far in these last fifty years. Different groups take themselves for granted to the point that they are demanding, for instance in the universities (and I am very much in sympathy with these demands), that recognition should be given not only to European and Western cultures, but also to all the other cultures that have fed into and are now feeding into the United States. Unfortunately, too often this approach to the relationship between the European and other groups focuses mainly on the multiplicity of cultures, rather than also on the recognition of the value of the individual without reference to race, or creed, or gender, or religion and nationality.

It is indeed a sign of progress that the rights of minorities are sufficiently recognized for them to make demands, even for special treatment in the light of past discrimination. The thing that worries me is that something we were emphasizing in 1946 and that Whitman emphasizes in his *Democratic Vistas* is being lost. I drew on Whitman particularly to set forth the importance of pluralism. This meant recognizing the worth of each man and woman as a unique individual, hence that each individual's own heritage must be respected. But at the same time, Whitman emphasized—even he who was a tremendously strong individualist—the fact that the individual, in order to be an individual, must have a unified society that provides the conditions of freedom for individuality and freedom for each group to persist in its own special way of life. Today they tend to take for granted the democratic society, the common understanding of democratic principles, that makes multicultural equality possible. We need to nourish the warm appreciation of diversity, but pride in our own heritage must not translate into hostility or mere competitiveness toward the different. We need to stress also our common human values and our common need to build a democratic society that protects and maintains our special identities as groups and as individuals, the kind of society that makes that multicultural emphasis constructive.

MARY: I can relate to what you are saying as I have grown up in Quebec. We have tensions about language, culture, and identity and separateness here in Canada and Quebec as well. I believe that you sat on a commission called the Human Relations Commission. What would you say to English teachers today about their role, given the concerns you have just expressed.

LOUISE: Yes. First of all, there is the whole problem of language. That is the business of recognizing that language is the very lifeblood of any group, of any society. Many differences stem from the fact that initially these multicultural groups do not speak the same language. On the one hand, we as teachers need to help youngsters respect and be proud of the language of the home and the language of their ethnic heritage. On the other hand, we have to make sure that youngsters also possess the common language, the language that will enable members of that group to participate in the common multicultural, pluralistic society that exists. I would prefer to say democratic society. It seems to me that both of these emphases are needed. We teachers of English have had a feeling of guilt about our former zeal to instill English. When I started fifty-six years ago, well-meaning teachers were really making youngsters ashamed of their family's language. Today, in reaction against an excessively narrow prescriptive concentration on technical correctness, there is the tendency to go to the other extreme and dwell mainly on the students' right to their own language. As educators and especially as English teachers, we have to also make sure that our students enter into and possess a common language. (Obviously the language is going to change as all the diverse elements enter into it. It's amusing to see what terms have come into the language in the last fifty years that have been drawn from different minority groups.) Change is part of the life of language. I found I was disturbed when an effort was made in some states to pass a law making English the official language in the United States, and it became apparent that, although the negative attitude toward minority languages had changed, our profession had not worked out a rounded position on the question.

MARY: You are referring to Hayakawa and the English Only Movement.

LOUISE: Yes, although I do not want to spend time on that particular organization, I do not believe that the point is English only but the need to work actively to maintain a common language. Both the National Council of Teachers of English and the Modern Language Association, two groups after all that should be most keenly aware of what the problem is, passed resolutions attacking the proposed law affirming English as the official language for various reasons. Largely I think because they were afraid it would be used in some way as a weapon against minority groups and against bilingual education. That happened, I believe, when such a law was passed in California. Nevertheless, I was concerned that these groups did not sufficiently realize that there was a problem—that there is a need for a common language, that we cannot be complacent about it, that the old processes may not work under present conditions. The Hayakawa group may not have provided the solution, but they were indicating that a problem exists. How do we continue to be a nation with a common language? That is very much the responsibility of the schools. As teachers of English, we have to work out, on the one hand, our acceptance and fostering of the value of the rich multicultural heritages feeding into our own multicultural society. At the same time, we have to be sure that we are providing not only a common language, but a common recognition of essential democratic values. In order to preserve that democratic way of life for all of us, we have to help youngsters understand and value it. So teachers of English have that dual responsibility: to help the child acquire the English language while remaining proud of his or her native heritage, and to develop the sense of a democratic way of life, democratic values that make it possible for us to honor and respect one another.

MARY: As you were talking, the metaphor that came to mind was one of "delicate balance," one that Elody Rathgen used in her interview in which she addressed the issues from a New Zealander's perspective and how English teachers are trying to accommodate cultural pluralism and the majority language and literature in that country. There are not too many countries where multiculturalism does not exist. I also see in many countries a push toward a unified curriculum such as Henrietta Dombey describes in Britain or E. D. Hirsch pushes forth in his notion of a canon of English studies.

LOUISE: Well, can I build up to that?

MARY: You can build up to it in any way you want.

LOUISE: You are about two jumps ahead of my own line of thought. You mention the image that came up in your mind. Well, again I think back to 1946. The image associated with the emphasis on assimilation to the dominant WASP model was the melting pot, which suggests homogenization of differences. The image Horace Kallen used for cultural pluralism was "orchestration," with each instrument in the orchestra contributing its own special voice. There is diversity within unity. The philosopher, John Dewey, wrote Kallen a letter and said, Yes, I like your idea of cultural pluralism as orchestration, if what is produced is a *symphony.* Dewey felt that assimilation to one another—not to the English strain—was essential; each cultural group should maintain its literary and artistic traditions in order to contribute to the others. Cultural pluralism accepts the existence of differences, but within a common—hence pluralistic—culture. "American" includes all the intermingled ethnic strains.

The recent positive affirmations of group and ethnic identities have unfortunately sometimes brought with them prejudice directed by one minority or ethnic group against another. Sometimes this is fueled by economic competition, but often the very prejudices blind them to their common economic interest. There is practical importance in stressing the goal of the symphony, commonalty as well as diversity. That's what is lacking, I believe, in the thinking today. People do not worry enough about the symphony. I came across another metaphor, a definition of democracy by Ralph Ellison. (I happened to meet him the other day and, as I had not located it in his *Invisible Man* or his essays, I asked him where he had said it. He said he couldn't remember.) What he said was that democracy was like a jazz band, each person cultivating his or her uniqueness yet harmonizing with the others.

That idea of democracy—that image of individuality—brings me back to what I was saying earlier about Whitman's building his vision of democracy on the belief in the importance of the individual. I have noted, for example, that for college students identification with other members of their ethnic or minority group provides support. But there is a tendency sometimes for the group to be jealous of other affiliations or participation in the mainstream. If people are all going to be identified mainly by their group membership, then that's fencing them in. I don't want to be fenced in. I belong to so many different groups: I am a woman, I am a Jew, I am aged, I am a senior citizen, I belong to a political party, to community and professional organizations; I have all sorts of interests in literary, musical groups, and so on. I don't want to be hemmed into any one of these groups. It seems to me that individuals of our society should be able to be proud of their ethnic backgrounds, but should also be free individuals and be able to identify also with other groups in which people of different ethnic backgrounds cooperate. It is the image of a freely harmonizing society that we as teachers of English constantly need to support.

Now you have also spoken of a national curriculum. That to my mind will be a tragedy unless teachers and all of us constantly see to it that people who impose that kind of curriculum understand what really goes on in a classroom. It's not uniformity, or a lock-step sequence, or rigid goals for each level that a national curriculum should provide, but some shared understanding of the conditions for constructive learning and teaching that will ensure the individual student's progress toward developmental goals. And one of those goals should be continuous growth in critical understanding of shared democratic values such as we have been discussing. But if mass quantitative methods of testing are continued, they would continue to dictate classroom activities, counteracting any national curriculum, no matter how enlightened.

MARY: What does this mean for the kinds of texts English teachers should or might bring into their classrooms?

LOUISE: Well, I took my doctorate in comparative literature and although I have always been in English departments, in my classes students have always read a great many texts in translation. They would read in the original when they could of course. I'm relating your question to the contemporary call for multicultural representation, when you probably were thinking in broader terms. Certainly, the notion of a single list of books to be read by all disregards all of the diversities—not only ethnic—that characterize our vast nation. Actually, the effort to draw on the wide ethnic range now present in our society would also apply to your broader question about the texts brought into English classrooms: no matter what other considerations enter into the choice of texts, they should offer something that the child can latch onto, link up with. I'm not thinking of "reading level" alone. (It's amazing, as you know, that when there is interest, a sense of connectedness, kids can read a text much above their supposed level and get something valuable from it, even though they will be able to do it greater justice in a later reading.) I'm thinking of the importance at all times and at all levels that the student should be involved, linking the new meanings, the new experiences to past understandings and experiences. That is sometimes another reason, besides the affirmation of identity, for providing texts that treat their ethnic background. However, that doesn't mean that only the specifics of their world provide such links. The texts from which they can evoke the basic human situations and emotional and intellectual experiences can provide the bridge to new understandings and broadened horizons.

Although I'm fearful of the rigidity of a national curriculum, there should be some shared literary experiences, I believe, because that is a kind of bonding important for the democratic orchestration or unity we were talking about earlier. (Note that I speak of experiences, not of odd bits of information and labels such as Hirsch lists.) The works need not be masterpieces; it's the sharing that's important. (What pleasure a friend and I, from very different backgrounds, had the other day over recollections of childhood reading of Whittier's "Snowbound"—no great masterpiece, surely!) Mother Goose, folk tales, the Bible, *Gulliver's Travels, Treasure Island, Huckleberry Finn,* and Shakespeare and Don Quixote still seem to be performing that function for many. As we develop a broader literary base from which to draw, I hope that this principle of shared experience will still play a role, although it should be applied with regard for individual and group readiness.

The calls for multicultural selection of texts usually stress the self-esteem children will derive from stories, say, about their own ethnic group. That is important. But equally important is the potentiality of literary experience to foster the mutual respect of different ethnic groups, the sense of connectedness with one another through the parallels as well as differences to be found in the diverse literature. And most important of all is the bond of their participating in the American society. They all share in the enveloping culture, to which they all contribute. And when even we think of the writers today who have emerged from a particular ethnic background, a Saul Bellow or a Toni Morrison—what a mixed literary heritage each actually represents!

All of this indicates the importance of making a wide range of texts available to students, but texts alone are not the answer. Texts are indeed important in the transaction. But I don't believe that texts should be thought of simply as didactic means to produce a certain multicultural effect. Transaction with the text provides the literary experience, but the school and the teacher are needed to create the climate and the guidance that will foster reflection and critical thinking.

When the matter of multiculturalism came up, a student said, "Why should we have to read their heritage when they don't read ours?" It's the divisiveness of "theirs" and "ours" that must be counteracted. They have to be helped to understand that all of us share the plural American heritage, which all of us will shape for future generations. So far as the reading of literature is concerned, we need to know why we are reading—that it is not simply to accept whatever image of life is presented in those works. One of the things that Whitman pointed out was that, although we want to derive inspiration from all the great literatures and all of the heritages, Eastern and Western, much of that literature was produced under conditions very different from ours. Take for example the image of women in the masterpieces of various literatures. Many rest on social and economic assumptions far from those of a democratic society. And that holds for the works produced in the European as well as other cultures.

One youngster, the child of recent immigrants, when told that George Washington was the "father of your country," replied, "He was no father of mine." The student needed to be helped to understand how he indeed participated in Washington's legacy, even if there were things in our society that he felt to be unjust. He needed to understand that Washington had repudiated much in his own British colonial background. From the very beginning, there has been built into the American life a critical attitude towards one's heritage and that's the attitude that we want to have in thinking about our familial heritage—what we want to save out of the heritage. What is it that is no longer in harmony with, in keeping with, or appropriate for American recognition of the value of all human beings and all heritages? It's that critical attitude, that discrimination, that sense that there are values to be applied, that must be built into the teaching of language and literature. Particularly in literary experience that becomes necessary and certainly possible, and that's of course what I have been preaching for fifty years.

I am quite aware of the many economic, political, and social factors in the present situation in the United States that make it difficult for such critical attitudes to develop. Too often it is the sense of past and present discrimination that holds the group together, and any self-criticism is felt to be disloyal. Yet real self-interest would be served by such discrimination of predispositions to resist, and positive values to be developed. Again, give-and-take, diversity within unity, should prevail within the various groups, as well as in the culturally plural democratic society as a whole.

MARY: How do you see teachers concretely accomplishing this harmonizing in a classroom?

LOUISE: Well, the reason why I'm so reluctant to talk about the business of a national curriculum is that, in order to talk about schools, we really have to talk about the economic and social situation in each country. At present, the schools are in many instances being called on to repair the damage due to the poverty and ignorance into which many children are born. In the United States, these demands on the schools are in general accompanied by low financial support and low esteem for teachers. Reforms being debated seem to me mainly palliative. But this is a complex question that requires more time than we can give to it here—except to explain why I think that, despite these overarching economic and social and political problems, it is important to work on such matters as learning theory and reading and literary theory. Even if all the socioeconomic and political conditions were ideal, if the teacher doesn't understand the long-term effect of what goes on in his or her classroom, there's not going to be really good education.

MARY: How do we bring about change?

LOUISE: I think of the kind of change Janet Emig has initiated, as well as the National Writing Project people or the California Literature Project. They are working directly with teachers to develop the personal understanding needed to do the kind of job that needs to be done. Maybe we can then become a strong political group. We need to have a clear understanding of the kind of job we need to be doing. For constructive change, two things have to begin at the same time. On the one hand, we try to do what each of us can as citizens to influence the economic, social, and political conditions that surround our schools. On the other hand, we have to be working toward helping teachers to liberate themselves from routine ways of thinking, to the point where they can in turn do the job of liberating students.

MARY: This reminds me of a letter I just received from Janet Emig. She mentions that one of her concerns is what she refers to as the balkanization of English studies and, in particular, literary studies. She says that we have had movements such as New Criticism, Marxism, Poststructuralism,

Postmodernism, and now of course the big push for Feminism. She expresses her concerns about limiting world views.

LOUISE: Yes, I agree. It happens because of excessive concentration on one issue and because of the tendency for the group to be jealous of ties to other groups. And I do not agree that the teacher should indoctrinate a particular "ism." Sometimes I think of writing an autobiography with the title *Don't Fence Me In.* I have been fenced in as one of the earliest to produce what is called today "reader-response critical theory." But in this group, for instance in one of the anthologies, you find people who are psychoanalytical, Marxist, feminists, deconstructionists, and of course I don't want to be fenced in with all of them. Nor do I want to be fenced in with those who understand reader-response as simply expression of personal feeling. Hence my insistence on the "transactional" label.

I find again that it is necessary to emphasize the importance of a multiplicity of approaches to the literary experience. What I want to emphasize is that whatever critical attitude you may apply, whether it be feminist, or Marxist, or what have you, the youngster should be enabled first of all to have a personal literary experience. The teacher needs to understand that youngsters are not reading to satisfy the teacher's particular approach, but they are reading in terms of their own needs and interests which they bring to the text and the literary experience, and they should be permitted to read in those terms. That is only the starting point of the educative process of learning to read critically. But this is a long developmental process, not a matter of a particular ideology imposed by the teacher. That simply leaves students vulnerable to demagoguery.

The teacher's role is to help the youngsters reflect on the literacy experience and, in terms of their own reactions and preoccupations, to become aware of the implicit underlying cultural and social assumptions of an evoked work. As youngsters hear what others have made of a text, they start to see that there are other possibilities in that text, and they can go back and become self-critical of their own reading of that text and scrutinize their own assumptions and values. The trouble with what Janet Emig calls the balkanization of English studies is that those folks—feminists, Marxists, structuralists, formalists, postmodernists—too often try to impose their particular stance or. concerns on the youngster. Youngsters should, at appropriate developmental times, become aware of alternative approaches, their strengths and limitations. The individual reader should feel free to have a personal literary experience as the foundation for personal growth. This should be the underlying principle. The only indoctrination should be of the democratic principles of the value and the freedom of human beings, as the framework for assessing alternative solutions to problems.

MARY: Many of the recent issues of *College English* include articles from a feminist perspective and argue that women have different ways of knowing, writing, learning, teaching. What's your view?

LOUISE: Well, that question would require detailed comments on specific theorists as they differ in many ways. On the whole, I agree as to the past, but am concerned that this emphasis might confirm stereotypes for the future. What I feel in all of this is a kind of pendulum swing to have different Englishes. So it is with the gender, race, ethnicity, or class emphasis. There is a tendency of a particular group to overemphasize a particular concern whether it be feminism or Marxism. At the moment, there is an overemphasis on diversity. Any cause, no matter how good it is, if a person becomes obsessed by it, then it becomes the one criterion by which to view everything else, and that is dangerous to a democratic society.

I am the mother of a son who is no male chauvinist, and the wife of a man who is an ardent feminist with whom I have had a shared life of common values and experiences. I can't see this tremendous emphasis on differences as more than a perhaps inevitable reaction against past discrimination. Of course there are differences between men and women. I see these just as I see literary and nonliterary, aesthetic and nonaesthetic, not as opposites but as a continuum. So it is with men and women. There is a continuum of traits, and most of the differences I believe are socially created and, if undesirable, can be modified or eliminated. Take feminism at the moment. As their definition of male or female, many still accept the patriarchal, culturally indoctrinated images of males and females, and they don't see that the image doesn't fit reality. There are men in our culture who are much closer to the so-called feminine and women to the so-called masculine. I certainly don't see it as a simple case of innate or absolute differences. Of course, many of the feminists to whom you refer understand this. Perhaps, we should try to develop non-gender-related terms for the various traits or styles.

MARY: Do you think that women read and write texts differently than men do?

LOUISE: In our culture, that may be so. But how much is due to degree of individual assimilation of cultural emphases, and how much to innate differences? I think that individuals read texts differently. I think that every reading is unique. Each reading is an event. Because of course even when you and I read the same text at different times, we read differently because we have had intervening experiences and different contexts for reading. We have had different experiences with reading Shakespeare at different times in our lives. All of this applies to writing, too, of course. On the other hand, there is much that we have in common, and literature I believe helps us to escape from our own limitations, whether it is gender, race, class, or religion, and experience the world through the eyes of others as well as our own. That's the value of literature to me or at least a basic value—that we can enlarge our horizons.

But on the other hand, society is made up of individuals, and the only way to make society better is to encourage individuals to see the result of their choices. So what I think we have to constantly do is to help people develop their imaginations and to see the result of their choices. We have to constantly help people discriminate what it is that they value and what it is that needs to be fostered and what it is that needs to be rejected. One needs to select out of one's experiences—as with one's heritage—and decide what one wants to preserve.

MARY: Your whole theory of literature is built on selective attention that is sometimes conscious and sometimes unconscious. We are moving increasingly in our lives to an information overload society. I think of Richard Eberhart's poem "Aerial Bombardment." What do you think we need to ferret out or eliminate?

LOUISE: Certainly, one of the first things to eliminate is old hatreds that are the result of the past and obstruct the present and future, to ferret out notions of superiority based on irrelevant things such as color, race, gender, ethnicity. It is important not only to ferret out those things, but to emphasize the positive, such as the value of the individual. A teacher recently told me that she had usually had classes of thirty-five students, but now she had only twenty students. Suddenly everything was improved. For instance, when a child was absent, everyone noticed it. The child begins to feel important. I could extrapolate from that anecdote a discussion of all the things that need to be eliminated from our educational system—from economic considerations to teaching methods to theory of reading, et cetera. But it would require much more time than we have.

MARY: That's the critical issue in all of this. You have talked about emphasizing the importance of creating symphonies. You used the analogy of children harmonizing in the classroom and respecting diversity. What do you think of Stanley Fish's notion of interpretive communities?

LOUISE: Yes, well he has really run that term into the ground. He himself has never consistently defined what he means by interpretive communities. He says that it is interpretive communities, rather than the text or the reader, that produce meanings and formal features. He says you are always limited by the strategies of your particular interpretive community, although at the same time he tries to persuade you to adopt his. I am at present writing a commentary on contemporary literary theories in which I point out that Fish's static, theoretical formulations do not provide for the process of change. I believe that my transactional theory, which recognizes the fluidity and newness of each coming-together of reader and text and context, explains how change and growth can happen during and after the reading (or writing) event. Although I agree on the need for shared criteria of interpretation, I don't believe that individuals are caught in the prison houses of their languages and cultures. So this whole notion that the individual is trapped in a particular interpretive community becomes irrelevant if we can present to the student an array of possible interpretive communities. One interpretive community such as the structuralists emphasizes structure almost to the exclusion of meaning. Another may emphasize let's say economic aspects to the exclusion of the whole experience and so on. We can start to see both the positive and the negative, the lacks in each of these approaches.

It is true that each of us has an internalized culture, that is, tacitly acquired ways of looking at the world. But in our twentieth century world, those cultures are constantly being impinged upon by other cultures. They are not fixed or static. Because of the mobility of people, in almost every country we are suddenly finding many different ethnic groups represented in many different places. As anthropologists know, every immigrant brings his or her own culture pattern into the host culture. We come to know what our own emphases are when we look at different cultures. Actually, the whole cultural picture is changing; we can look at our Western culture against a Buddhist culture. We can begin to see the values in our culture that are stressed and those stressed by Buddhists. We can accept some from the other culture and discard some of our own. Marginal cultures have always changed as they have come into contact with other cultures.

Actually, we're no longer prisoners as I see it of our own culture or ethnicity. To the extent that we have a common language we can, not necessarily abandon our own heritage or denigrate it, we can be proud of it. But we can enter into the broader society and see what we can contribute that's valuable, and what of our own past has changed. For instance, in the Jewish heritage the position of women has changed tremendously in the thinking of most of the members of that ethnic group today as against the past. All cultures can change, particularly as they intermingle with others. Looking back to recapture roots has its values, but to focus on the future, on creating a new and better society, would be invigorating.

If we had that kind of an image, then the same applies to the idea of interpretive community. I mean there are moments when I find it interesting to read a structuralist analysis of a poem, fixated on static concepts of form. I think it's usually very sterile, but at the same time it does emphasize certain things that then I may want to be more aware of when I myself go back to what I consider a more humanistic way of looking at the literary experience. So it's that kind of understanding of interpretive I see. I would not say community because again that's insular; it's like this notion that language is a kind of self-contained system that's writing us.

MARY: Is that why you insist so strongly on the term *transaction* rather than *interaction?*

LOUISE: Language is something that is made; it is created out of human lives, out of human use. I use the term *transaction* to designate mutual, reciprocal relationships. It's not an "interaction" between separate and distinct entities in a decontextualized void. It's an interflowing interfusion that goes on between us and the environment, between us and other people. We're constantly affecting and being affected by the world around us. So the notion of a static, rigid language holding us in is just not true to reality. I remember Professor Boas saying that when I studied primitive linguistics with him. I remember him saying that there's no language that he knew of that cannot create a new word or assimilate a new idea.

MARY: It's the whole notion that language is generative.

LOUISE: Yes indeed, as individuals transact with it in changing situations. Now, my objection to the notion of the absolute control of language does not deny the great importance of language. For example, note my insistence on the importance of the different implications of the terms *melting pot, cultural pluralism,* and *multiculturalism.* It's true that there are implicit metaphors that we have to be sensitive to, but that's what we as teachers can help youngsters become aware of. I do not think of our concern being primarily or only literature, by the way. When I speak of the efferent (the nonaesthetic) and the aesthetic reading, I think it's just as important for us to understand a piece of writing about economics as to have had experience in sensing and analyzing literary, aesthetic experiences.

The point is that we have to manage both cognitive and affective elements in either kind of reading—it's the "mix" that's different and the two kinds of purpose require different kinds of evaluation. Learning to critically read aesthetically can help in reading nonaesthetically, and vice versa. The economist or the scientist tends to use metaphors that affect us, often without our being aware of it. Someone may write about fascism as the wave of the future, wanting us to feel that it is irresistible, but we must react critically. So it's just as important for us to be teaching nonliterary as literary reading. But we have to recognize that these are not oppositions and that there's a continuum. In order to read the nonliterary, you have to be sensitive to the aesthetic aspects of the nonliterary experience just as much as you may have to be sensitive to and evaluate the logical, or rational, or factual implications of your literary experience.

MARY: It's the stance that the reader chooses at a particular moment. You started with that notion in *Literature as Exploration.*

LOUISE: And of course the reader by choosing an efferent or an aesthetic stance is deciding to pay attention more to one aspect of the contents of consciousness than another. In other words the logical and factual aspects are always there, but the sensuous, and the associative, and the imagery aspects are there too. It's a question of what you're going to pay attention to. When somebody talks about the decline of American society, for instance, obviously we should be thinking about, well: What are the facts? But then we also have to think: Do those facts justify that particular metaphor of decline? Maybe it's a needed stabilization. In other words you have to learn how to handle those different aspects of linguistic experience. The efferent, or nonaesthetic and the aesthetic are a continuum. Most of the time we're sort of in the middle and we have to handle both aspects and we have to decide what is our dominant, our main purpose. If the main purpose is practical and factual and logical, we have to learn how to subordinate even the aesthetic aspect for that particular moment.

MARY: So you assign a strong role to reader intentionality?

LOUISE: Very much so. That's what the child has to be helped to see. Children should have learned this without being given the theory. Just the whole environmental handling in the classroom should help them to feel when they're reading for information and when they're reading for a new experience. My favorite is the account of the youngster who became interested in dinosaurs. So his teacher gave him books on dinosaurs and he was very much dissatisfied. He said, "These are storybooks. I want to know about dinosaurs." He knew the difference between efferent and aesthetic reading. He was happy to read those stories, but they had raised the question in his mind, "Well, I wonder what dinosaurs really were like?" And that's what he wanted to know, and both of those ways of thinking and reading need to go on in the English classroom.

MARY: Yes. There are dinosaurs and there are dinosaurs.

LOUISE: I recall one young woman who read Tolstoy's *Anna Karenina* and passed harsh judgments on the characters and on the novel, and then she suddenly discovered that she was judging that whole nineteenth century Russian situation in terms of the present, and ultimately that she couldn't extrapolate the situation to the present because of lack of knowledge. So that was evidence of a very fruitful, active reading of that novel.

MARY: You're making a very strong case, as you have always, for making students aware of the implicit, tacit cultural and social and political assumptions that a work will evoke at any one time.

LOUISE: Evocation, the living-through of the evoked work, is the key word in this whole process since the student had arrived at such insights into the complexities of moral judgment through a process of self-criticism. Understanding had developed from, was rooted in, lived-through personal—aesthetic—experience. That's very different from simply following a teacher's assignment to analyze a work from a social or historical point of view. As we have been speaking about the various issues you have raised, I have assumed largely that there was little need to elaborate on all the problems facing American society and the global society. It's ironic, in a way, that I share with other postmodern theorists the understanding that there are no absolute answers, that there are conflicts of interest and power, yet I do not share their tendency to overemphasize uncertainty, to approach the society and even the text with skepticism and pessimism. Perhaps longevity does provide perspective, since I've seen the decline of successive "hegemonic" movements. I started my scholarly career with study of nineteenth century *fin de siècle* "decadence" and pessimism. Coincidentally, now at the end of a century sees a surge of negativism, but I can find the courage to assert not only the need but also the reasonableness of seeking humane, democratic solutions. I feel it important to stress confidence in tentative pragmatic solutions to the quest for certainty both in interpretation and in the world.

Selected Bibliography
for Louise M. Rosenblatt

L'Idée de l'art pour l'art dans la litterature anglaise pendant la période victorienne. 1931. Paris: H. Champion.

Literature as Exploration. 1938. New York: D. Appleton Century. 1983, 3rd edition. New York: Langauge Association of America.

The Reader, the Text, the Poem: The Transactional Theory of the Literary Work. 1978. Carbondale: Southern Illinois University; 1994, paperback edition with epilogue.

Viewpoints: Transaction versus Interaction—A Terminological Rescue Operation. 1985. *Research in the Teaching of English, 19(1),* 96-107.

The Transactional Theory of Reading and Writing. 1994. In *Theoretical Models and Processes of Reading* (4th edition), edited by R. B. Ruddell, M. L. Ruddell, and H. Singer, 1057-1092. Newark, Del.: International Reading Association.

Epilogue: Continuing the Dialogue

C ertain common motifs run through these conversations—which is interesting, given the very different educational and political realities for all these women scholars who participated in this international dialogue. Conferences from Dartmouth on have pointed to fundamental differences in stance and philosophy as one crosses the Atlantic and then again the Pacific. However, the commonalties here may well reflect, as Aviva Freedman says, that I selected these women (and not others) to interview at a particular moment in time. Or there may be indeed certain gender-related orientations, despite other very significant differences in cultural, political, and ideological settings. Yetta Goodman sees the power of definition as central to her reading of these conversations and how these women explore issues that highlight optimism, potential, and possibilities as they define and redefine themselves.

As I revisited their texts, intertexts, and the social, personal situatedness of their contexts, I sensed a rich mixture of personal values, purposes, and ages that resonates within and across their voices. Bakhtin's concept of utterance as dialogic and situated activity is evident in these intertwined conversations. These women articulate commonalties. But they also articulate different understandings of their social situatedness through their use of language and positioning themselves within their particular contexts. Elody Rathgen believes that "these reflections sum up the place each woman was at during the time of the interview, but leave a sense of ongoing concerns of the never-ending fascination of learning about and through language."

Aviva refers to negative capability and humility to characterize the motifs and stances she sees in these intertwined conversations. Margaret Gill revisits the concept of empowerment and cautions us that it now feels like other concepts such as critical literacy, critical pedagogy, and cultural literacy, yet another buzz word that has lost its valency. She emphasizes that "empowerment to participate most fully in society is not an automatic consequence of even the most effective critical pedagogy." In Louise Rosenblatt's view, this is especially true when certain orientations are privileged over others. Margaret Meek Spencer appreciates my intertextual initiative and sees our conversations as continuing, fluid dialogues over time and not as bounded texts. The discourses ebb and flow in her view, and I hope for readers as well. Elody also sees the dialogues as fluid, the ideas and topics as not finished business. This fluidity and recursiveness of language use and thinking was what I hoped to capture in each conversation. As stories beget stories, so may conversations beget further conversations.

Henrietta Dombey reminds us of the ebb and flow we experience between optimism and pessimism in our professional lives as English teachers, and I would add female scholars. Janet Emig and Elody confront squarely the issues of power and attribution in the academy and the profession. Nowhere have I seen that played out so blatantly than at the 1986 conference at Carleton. As chair of the research strand for the conference on "Issues That Unite or Divide Us" as a profession, I felt the electricity in the audience as we listened to the debate between Janet and Carl Bereiter on research paradigms and different ways of knowing. In her interview for this book, Margaret Meek Spencer offers for me the advice that "the best thing one does in education is to be honest with one's colleagues, to take them into one's thinking, and to expect honest responses." Certainly as editor, I know that this book was constructed because of relationships of mutual trust and respect for self and others.

What does this mean for English teachers and their students? Patricia Symmonds talks about changing the balance in the English curriculum, and Elody refers to the whole process as a delicate balance. She asks us to think about whose interests are being served as we develop our pedagogies of reading, writing, and acting. We may well ask whose stories are being told or not, whose stories in the narrative conversational exchange are getting the floor or not, which narrators are being heard, listened to, and understood or not. Louise Rosenblatt gives us new metaphors for conceptualizing and living within our professional communities and classrooms: "It is the image of a freely harmonizing society that we as teachers of English need to support." Louise believes that "people don't worry enough about the symphony." I am certainly very aware of the potential voices such as African and Asian women whom I did not have the opportunity to tap and include in this version of *Dialogue in a Major Key*. Margaret Gill says that "things need to be said differently. Things are different." New voices are needed to enter the conversational circle to help us understand these differences.

Does all this add up to a typically female stance? Certainly a number of scholars such as Aviva Freedman and Janet Emig make this connection, although I did not deliberately or consciously set out to do this when I interviewed these women. Janet defines the female principle as "more willing to trust the expressive mode" and consequently to listen to and trust the expression of others, as well as to trust the storying—with its modes of inquiry and representation. My experiences with the logistics of constructing this book and the conversations and dialogues about and surrounding it as a text have broadened my understanding of the interrelationships of texts and contexts. The diversity among the faxes, letters, telephone calls, exchanges of ideas, opinions and information, and dinner table conversations related to this book have also given me a new appreciation of the multiple possibilities of dialogic forms and forums of inquiry and representation in the art of opening conversations and keeping the dialogue going.

What does this mean for our traditional concept of book as text? The title *Dialogue in a Major Key* and the contents of intertwined conversations invite speculation for those interested in typological approaches to discourse. I leave that to those who are interested in that line of inquiry. I am aware that I sometimes use "dialogue" and "conversation" interchangeably. I leave you, the readers, with an invitation to enter and engage with this text, the intertexts, the conversations, to bring your own experiences to them and make your own connections and create your own conversations.

Louise Rosenblatt emphasizes that "the transactional view places the stress on each reading as a particular event, involving a particular reader and a particular text under particular circumstance." She says that "a text derives its life from the stream of readers who incorporate the texts into the changing matrix of their lives." If I had been asked the question—What made me construct this text?—I wonder what I might have said. I now know that what I want is further dialogue.

Abbreviations for Organizations

AATE: Australian Association for the Teaching of English

CCCC: Conference on College Composition and Communication, also known as four C's (constituent organization of NCTE)

CCTE: Canadian Council of Teachers of English (now called CCTELA: Canadian Council of Teachers of English and Language Arts)

CEE: Conference on English Education (constituent organization of NCTE)

IFTE: International Federation for the Teaching of English

NATE: National Association for the Teaching of English

NCTE: National Council of Teachers of English

NZATE: New Zealand Association of Teachers of English

References

Adams, M. J. 1990. *Beginning to Read: Thinking and Learning about Print.* Cambridge, Mass.: MIT Press.

Bakhtin, M. 1981. Discourse in the Novel. In *The Dialogic Imagination: Four Essays,* edited by M. Holquist; translated by C. Emerson and M. Holquist, 259–422. Austin: University of Texas Press.

Barthes, R. 1973. Theory of the Text. In *Untying the Text: A Post-structualist Reader,* edited by R. Young; translated 1981. Boston: Routledge & Kegan Paul.

Bartholomae, D. 1985. Inventing the University. In *When a Writer Can't Write: Studies in Writer's Block and Other Composing-Process Problems,* edited by M. Rose, 134–165. New York: Guilford Press.

Bartholomae, D., and A. Petrosky, eds. 1986. *Facts, Artifacts and Counterfacts: Theory and Method for a Reading and Writing Course.* Upper Montclair, N.J.: Boynton/Cook.

Bazerman, C. 1989. *The Informed Writer: Using Sources in the Disciplines.* Boston: Houghton Mifflin.

Belenky, M. F., M. C. Blythe, N. R. Goldberger, and J. M. Tarule. 1986. *Women's Ways of Knowing: The Development of Self, Voice, and Mind.* New York: Basic Books.

Benedict, R. 1934. *Patterns of Culture.* Boston: Houghton Mifflin.

Bereiter, C., and M. Scardamalia. 1982. From Conversation to Composition: The Role of Instruction in a Developmental Process. In *Advances in Instructional Psychology* (vol. 2), edited by R. Glaser, 1-64. Hillsdale, N.J.: Lawrence Erlbaum.

Britton, J. 1970. *Language and Learning.* Harmondsworth, England: Penguin Books (2nd ed. 1992).

Bruffee, K. A. 1984. Collaborative Learning and the "Conversation of Mankind." *College English, 46(7),* 635-652.

Bruner, J. 1986. *Actual Minds, Possible Worlds.* Cambridge, Mass.: Harvard University Press.

Buber, M. 1958. *I and Thou,* translated by R. Gregor Smith. New York: Charles Scribner's Sons.

Bullock, A. 1975. *A Language for Life.* London: Her Majesty's Stationary Office.

Clifford, J. 1988. *The Predicament of Culture: Twentieth-Century Ethnography, Literature and Art.* Cambridge, Mass.: Harvard University Press.

Csikszentmihalyi, M., and R. Larson. 1984. *Being Adolescent.* New York: Basic Books.

Department of Employment, Education and Training. 1991. *Australia's Language: The Australian Language and Literacy Policy.* Canberra: Australian Government Publishing Service.

Dewey, J. 1916. *Democracy and Education: An Introduction to the Philosophy of Education.* New York: Macmillan.

———. 1959. *Art as Experience.* New York: Capricorn.

Dixon, J. 1967. *Growth through English: A Report Based on the Dartmouth Seminar, 1966* (2nd ed. 1969; 3rd ed. 1975). Reading, England: National Association for the Teaching of English.

Eagleton, T. 1983. *Literary Theory: An Introduction.* Minneapolis: University of Minnesota Press.

Elbow, P. 1990. *What Is English?* New York: Modern Language Association of America; Urbana, Ill.: National Council of Teachers of English.

Eliot, T. S. 1943. *Four Quartets.* New York: Harcourt, Brace & World.

Elliot, S. 1991–1992. *Whole Language Umbrella Newsletter, 3(1),* 1.

Emig, J. 1983. Inquiry Paradigms and Writing. In *The Web of Meaning: Essays on Writing, Teaching, Learning, and Thinking,* edited by D. Goswami and M. Butler, 157–170. Upper Montclair, N.J.: Boynton/Cook.

Ervin-Tripp, S. 1974. Is Second Language Learning Like the First? *TESOL Quarterly, 8(2),* 111–127.

Fairclough, N. 1989. *Language and Power.* Essex, U.K.: Longman.

Farrell, E. J., and J. R. Squire, eds. 1990. *Transactions with Literature: A Fifty-Year Perspective: For Louise M. Rosenblatt.* Urbana, Ill.: National Council of Teachers of English.

Fraser, R. 1984. *In Search of a Past: The Rearing of an English Gentleman.* New York: Atheneum.

Freedman, A., I. Pringle, and J. Yalden. 1983. *Learning to Write: First Language/ Second Language: Selected Papers from the 1979 CCTE Conference, Ottawa, Canada.* New York. Longman.

Freire, P. 1985. *The Politics of Education.* South Hadley, Mass.: Bergin and Garvey.

Gadamer, H. G. 1977. *Philosophical Hermeneutics,* edited and translated by D. E. Linge. Berkeley: University of California Press.

————. 1989. *Truth and Method.* New York: Crossroad.

Gardner, H. 1991. *The Unschooled Mind: How Children Think and How Schools Should Teach.* New York: Basic Books.

Geertz, C. 1973. *Interpretation of Cultures: Selected Essays.* New York: Basic Books.

Gilligan, C. 1982. *In a Different Voice: Psychological Theory and Women's Development.* Cambridge, Mass.: Harvard University Press.

Giroux, H. A. 1987. Cultural Literacy and Student Experience: Donald Graves' Approach to Literacy. *Language Arts, 64(2),* 175–181.

Goffman, E. 1959. *The Presentation of Self in Everyday Life.* Garden City, N.Y.: Doubleday.

Goodman, K. S. 1984. Unity in Reading. In *Becoming Readers in a Complex Society,* edited by A. C. Purves and O. Niles, 79–114. Chicago: The National Society for the Study of Education.

Goodman, Y. M., et al. 1991. Beginning to Read: A Critique by Literacy Professionals and a Response by Marilyn Jager Adams. *The Reading Teacher, 44(6),* 375–378.

Graves, D. H. 1983. *Writing: Teachers and Children at Work.* Exeter, N.H.: Heinemann.

Halliday, M. A. K. 1978. *Language as a Social Semiotic: The Social Interpretation of Language and Meaning.* Baltimore: University Park Press.

Heath, S. B. 1983. *Ways With Words: Language, Life, and Work in Communities and Classrooms.* New York: Cambridge University Press.

Hirsch, E. D., Jr. 1987. *Cultural Literacy: What Every American Needs to Know.* Boston: Houghton Mifflin.

Hymes, D. 1972. Models of the Interaction of Language and Social Life. In *Directions in Sociolinguistics: The Ethnography of Communication,* edited by J. J. Gumperz and D. Hymes, 35–71. New York: Holt, Rinehart and Winston.

International Literacy Secretariat. 1990. International Literacy Year Paper No. 1 (mimeograph).

Iser, W. 1978. *The Act of Reading: A Theory of Aesthetic Response.* Baltimore: Johns Hopkins University Press.

John-Steiner, V. 1985. *Notebooks of the Mind: Explorations of Thinking.* Albuquerque: University of New Mexico Press.

Kristeva, J. 1969. Semiotikè: Recherches pour une sémanalyse. Paris: Editions du Seuil.

Maguire, M. H. 1988. How Do They Tell? Ecrire c'est choisir. In *Language and Literacy in the Primary School,* edited by M. Meek and C. Mills, 235–247. London: Falmer Press.

———. 1989. Understanding and Implementing a Whole-Langauge Program in Quebec. *The Elementary School Journal, 90(2),* 143–160.

———. 1991. Epiphanies of the Ordinary: Playful Literacy Lessons and Playing within Literacy Lessons. *Reflections on Canadian Literacy, 9(1),* 40–49.

———. 1992. Context, Texts and Computers. *Journal of the Canadian Association of Applied Linguistics, 14(1),* 75–94.

———. 1994. Cultural Stances of Two Quebec Bilingual Children Informing Story Telling. *Comparative Education Review, 38(1),* 115–144.

Maguire, M. H., and J. Kniskern. 1989. National Policy Statement on Language Development and Early Literacy. Ottawa: Canadian Council of Teachers of English.

McDermott, R. P. 1987. The Explanation of Minority School Failure, Again. *Anthropology and Education Quarterly, 18,* 361–364.

Medway, P. 1980. *Finding a Language: Autonomy and Learning in School.* London: Writers and Readers in Association with Chameleon.

Meek, M. 1982. *Learning to Read.* London: The Bodley Head.

Michaels, S. 1981. Sharing Time: Children's Narrative Style and Differentiated Access to Literacy. *Language in Society, 10,* 423–442.

Miller, J. 1983. *Many Voices: Bilingualism, Culture, and Education.* London: Routledge and Kegan Paul.

Paley, V. G. 1981. *Wally's Stories.* Cambridge, Mass.: Harvard University Press.

———. 1989. *Must Teachers Also Be Writers?* Occasional Paper No. 13. Berkeley: University of California, Center for the Study of Writing.

Phelps, L. 1988. *Composition as a Human Science: Contributions to the Self-Understanding of a Discipline.* New York: Oxford University Press.

Philips, S. U. 1982. *The Invisible Culture: Communication in Classroom and Community on the Warm Springs Indian Reservation.* New York: Longman.

Pradl, G. M. 1979. Learning How to Begin and End a Story. *Language Arts, 56(1),* 21–25.

———, ed. 1982. *Prospect and Retrospect: Selected Essays of James Britton.* Montclair, N.J.: Boynton/Cook.

Pringle, I. 1983. English as a World Language—Right Out There in the Playground. In *Timely Voices: English Teaching in the Eighties,* edited by R. Arnold, 187–208. Melbourne: Oxford University Press.

Polanyi, M. l958. *Personal Knowledge.* London: Routledge and Kegan Paul.

Proust, M. 1954. *A la recherche du temps perdu.* Paris: Gallimard.

Reid, I. 1984. *The Making of Literature.* Adelaide: Australian Association for the Teaching of English.

Richards, I. A. 1929. *Practical Criticism.* London: Harcourt Brace.

Ricoeur, P. 1984. *Time and Narrative,* translated by K. McLaughlin and D. Pellauer. Chicago: University of Chicago Press.

Rorty, R. 1979. *Philosophy and the Mirror of Nature.* Princeton, N.J.: Princeton University Press.

Rose, M. 1989. *Lives on the Boundary: The Struggles and Achievements of America's Underprepared.* New York: Free Press.

Rosen, H. 1986. The Importance of Story. *Language Arts, 63(3),* 226–237.

Sapir, E. 1921. *Language, an Introduction to the Study of Speech.* New York: Harcourt Brace.

Scholes, R. 1988. Three Views of Education: Nostalgia, History and Voodoo. *College English, 50(31),* 323–332.

———. 1985. *Textual Power: Literary Theory and the Teaching of English.* New Haven, Conn.: Yale University Press.

Schon, D. A. 1987. *Educating the Reflective Practitioner: Toward a New Design for Teaching and Learning in the Professions.* San Francisco: Jossey-Bass.

Scribner, S., and M. Cole. 1981. *The Psychology of Literacy.* Cambridge, Mass.: Harvard University Press.

Steedman, C. 1982. *The Tidy House: Little Girls Writing.* London: Virago.

———. 1987. *Landscape for a Good Woman: A Story of Two Lives.* New Brunswick, N.J.: Rutgers University Press.

Sterne, L. 1940. *The Life and Opinions of Tristram Shandy, Gentleman.* New York: The Odyssey Press.

Tannen, D. 1989. *Talking Voices.* New York: Cambridge University Press.

———. 1990. *You Just Don't Understand: Women and Men in Conversation.* New York: Ballantine Books.

Taylor, D., and C. Dorsey-Gaines. 1988. *Growing Up Literate: Learning from Inner-City Families.* Portsmouth, N.H.: Heinemann.

Tizard, B., and M. Hughes. 1984. *Young Children Learning.* Cambridge, Mass.: Harvard University Press.

Wells, G. 1986. *The Meaning Makers: Children Learning Language and Using Language to Learn.* Portsmouth, N.H.: Heinemann.

Wertsch, J. V., ed. 1985. *Culture, Communication, and Cognition: Vygotskian Perspectives.* New York: Cambridge University Press.

Whitman, W. 1964. *Walt Whitman, Selected and with Notes by Mark van Doren.* New York: Viking Press.

Winnicott, D. W. 1971. *Playing and Reality.* London: Tavistock Publishers.

Worf, B. L. 1956. *Language, Thought and Reality; Selected Writings.* Cambridge, Mass.: MIT Press.

Index

Editor

Mary H. Maguire is associate professor in the Department of Education in Second Languages in the Faculty of Education at McGill University. A former secondary school English teacher, she focuses her research on bilingual children's biliteracy, language, and learning in multilingual and multicultural contexts. She has written about her work in many articles and book chapters and presented at many international conferences in Canada, the United Kingdom, and the United States. With Julie Kniskern, she co-authored the language development policy statement for the Canadian Council of Teachers of English. She also served as a member of the National Research Design and Research Coordinating Committee for the Canadian Education Association and Human Resources and Development Canada during a study of school success in Canadian secondary schools. More recently, she is the principal investigator for a study of the school success and biliteracy development of minority language elementary children in different bilingual programs in Montreal and Ottawa.

Contributors

Henrietta Dombey is principal lecturer in the Department of Primary Education at Brighton Polytechnic in England. During the first formulation of the National Curriculum, she was, as chair of the National Association of the Teaching of English, in a position to help teachers of English make their perceptions and ideas contribute to the process. She has served on a number of committees dealing with assessment, particularly of early literacy, and has published widely on children's reading, language, and literacy. Her presentations include conferences in the United States, Australia, and Canada, as well as in the United Kingdom.

Janet Emig has taught fourth grade through graduate school during the forty-two years of her teaching career. She retired from Rutgers University in the fall of 1991. She is past president of the National Council of Teachers of English. She is the author of the *Composing Process of Twelfth Graders* and *The Web of Meaning,* for which she received the Mina Shaughnessay medal from the Modern Language Association in 1983. In 1990 her undergraduate college, Mount Holyoke, awarded her an honorary Doctor of Humane Letters degree for serving as "the vanguard of a revolution in the theory and practice of writing instruction." She is currently editing a collection of her recent essays, *Field Notes from a Profession;* her own poetry, *The Cost of Living;* and two scholarly texts, in addition to writing her first mystery, *Death of a Reformer.*

Aviva Freedman is professor in the Department of Linguistics and Applied Language Studies at Carleton University. Her research has focused on development in writing abilities from childhood through the adult years. Currently she is studying the processes and products of learning to write at school and in the workplace from the dual perspectives of genre theory and activity theory. Numerous articles and chapters on these and related subjects have been published in Canada, the United Kingdom, and the United

States. She co-edited *Reinventing the Rhetorical Tradition* and *Learning to Write* with Ian Pringle, and *Learning and Teaching Genre* and *Genre in the New Rhetoric* with Peter Medway.

Margaret Gill is associate professor in the School of Graduate Studies Faculty of Education at Monash University, Clayton, Australia. She is past president of both the International Federation for the Teaching of English and the Australian Association for the Teaching of English. She has researched and published in the field of English curriculum and implementation. She has presented papers and delivered many keynote addresses at major conferences in Canada, Australia, the United States, and the United Kingdom.

Yetta M. Goodman is regents professor at the University of Arizona College of Education. In the Language, Reading and Culture Department, she teaches graduate and undergraduate courses in language and literacy development, miscue analysis, and reading and writing processes. For more than twenty-five years, she has been involved in research related to miscue analysis and literacy development. She is a prolific writer and international speaker. As an advocate of whole-language theory, she actively supports the rights of teachers to have decision-making power in their classrooms and has popularized the term *kid watching.* She is past president of the National Council of Teachers of English.

Elody Rathgen is past president of the International Federation for the Teaching of English. She teaches at Christchurch College of Education in Christchurch, New Zealand. She has served on numerous Ministry of Education curriculum committees and presented at many international conferences on issues of reading and gender in Canada, New Zealand, the United Kingdom, and the United States.

Louise M. Rosenblatt is professor emeritus at New York University. Her long and distinguished career as a teacher, researcher, and writer spans fifty years. She received her undergraduate degree at Barnard College and her doctorate at the University of Paris, and she did postdoctoral studies in anthropology at Columbia University. Her life work on a transactional approach to reader-response includes two books on literacy theory, *Literature as Exploration* and *The Reader, the Text, the Poem,* as well as numerous articles. These affirm her belief in the importance of individual reader-response for achieving one's potential in a democratic society.

Margaret Meek Spencer is a teacher, critic, and reviewer of children's books. In 1990, she received the Elena Farjeon award for her services to children and books. She wrote *Learning to Read,* a book that brought encouragement and support to thousands of parents by explaining what happens when a child is taught to read. Recently retired from her position as reader in education at the University of London Institute of Education, she continues to do research and to advise in the field of education and literacy. Among her many publications are *Adolescent Language and Literacy, Opening Moves, Language and Learning in the Primary School,* and *On Being Literate.*

Patricia Symmonds is former headmistress, deputy head, English teacher at the St. Michael School in Barbados. Since her retirement, she has continued to lecture to adult classes on the use of English and to be active in matters relating to education and the teaching of English. She was founding member and president of the Barbados Association for the Teaching of English and first president of the Caribbean Association for the Teaching of English. She was part-time lecturer in English for two years at the College of Arts and Science, now the Cave Hill Campus of the University of the West Indies. She has served on language arts curriculum committees for the Ministry of Education and the National Curriculum Development Council. Among her publications are *On Language and Life-Styles.*